Stories from
Rabindranath Tagore's Galpaguchha

Author
Rabindranath Tagore

Translation and Adaptation
Dipavali Sen

Publisher
UNICORN BOOKS

F-2/16, Ansari Road, Daryaganj, New Delhi-110002
☎ 011-23275434, 23262683, 23250704 • *Fax:* 011-23257790
E-mail: info@unicornbooks.in • *Website:* www.unicornbooks.in

ISBN 978-81-7806-365-2

Printed at : Param Offsetters, Okhla, New Delhi-110020.

Contents

An Introduction to One Who Needs None

Rabindrathnath Tagore (Thakur) was the first Asian to win the Nobel Prize(in 1913). A hundred years later, his charisma goes much beyond the Nobel Prize. He is called *Visva-kavi* (World-Poet) and is indeed among the world's greatest men.

Rabindranath Tagore was born on 7 May 1861 (`*Ponchishe Baishakh* to Bengalis) at Jorasanko in Kolkata to Devendranath Tagore and his wife Sarada.

The Tagores were an established family. Dwarakanath Tagore, the father of Devendranath Tagore (and so the grandfather of Rabindranath Tagore), had done business with the British on a partnership basis. The Carr-Tagore Company is one of the early examples of Indo-British joint venture. Dwarakanath also bought several pieces of land under the *zamindari* system (some pieces now falling in present Bangladesh) and travelled, extensively and for long, in Europe. For his luxurious and generous ways, the British called him `Prince Dwarakanath'. But he died rather early, leaving his son Devendranath Tagore a lot of landed property as well as a lot of business debts.

Young Devendranath paid off every pie of his inherited

debt and remained contented with the property that remained. He was of a spiritual cast of mind and a great enthusiast of the Brahmo Samaj movement pioneered by Raja Ram Mohun Roy (who contributed to the abolition of the *Sati-daha-pratha* or `Suttee'). Several of Devendranath Tagore's sons were illustrious personalities. His eldest son Dwijendranath Tagore was a well-known mathematician. Son Satyendranath Tagore was the first Indian I.C.S. Officer. And, as we all know, his youngest son Rabindranath Tagore went on to win the Nobel Prize. `Robi' (Ravi) as he was called, was brought up in a sprawling mansion in Jorasanko (now the premises of Rabindra Bharati University), but austerely. He was sent to a reputed local school but he found school atmosphere stifling. There was a creative genius within him waiting to burst out like the spring-water. Right at the age of eleven, he began to write poetry. Jyotirindranath Tagore, an elder brother (himself very talented) gave him a lot of encouragement in writing songs and plays. At the age of fourteen, Robi lost his mother, but his sister-in-law Kadambari, Jyotirindranath's wife, took him under her wings. She was a great inspiration for him and he acknowledged her even at a ripe old age.

Rabindranath sailed to England at the age of 17 and then again at the age of 21. By then he had blossomed into a poet and received praise from several important personages such as Bankim Chandra Chattopadhyaya, the novelist who gave India the song `*Vande Mataram*'.

In 1883 Rabindranath got married to Mrinalini Devi and entered domestic life. Soon after, his sister-in-law Kadambari Devi passed away. But in spite of domesticity and the loss of a source of inspiration,Rabindranath, with the poetry alive in his heart , kept on writing poems, short stories, novels, songs, plays and essays in an unending stream. In 1890, Devendranath sent him to look after their *zamindari* property on the banks of the river Padma (now in Bangladesh). Rabindranath proved to be an efficient but concerned *zamindar*. Also, he now came into contact with disadvantaged people in rural and interior areas to whom he had no earlier exposure.

This experience gave him ideas which he developed into creative literature: poems, short stories and novels. It also ignited an interest in rural development and economic issues. Rabindranath also took an interest in India's freedom movement and attended sessions of the Indian National Congress.

In December 1901, Rabindranath, then 41, set up a school for children at Santiniketan (Abode of Peace) in district Birbhum of West Bengal. It was so-called because Devendranath had found peace (*santi*) and quiet in this bit of land that he had in the Bengal-Bihar border region.

Rabindranath had visited it in his childhood and found its openness a refreshing change from his cooped-up condition in Kolkata. It was an open-air school in the model of *ashrams* of ancient India and was, in fact, originally called `Santiniketan Brahmacharyashrama'.

Soon, within the span of a few years, Rabindranath lost his wife, his father and younger son. Personal losses, however, did not hamper his creativity. With the publication of *Manasi* and *Sonar Tari* in 1890 and 94 respectively, as a poet he was a household name.

On the Partition of Bengal in 1905 by Lord Curzon, he protested in a unique way by walking along Kolkata streets singing his song `*Banglar Mati Banglar Jal*' (now the national anthem of Bangladesh) and tying *rakhis* to one and all. In 1910 in the novel *Gora* (Fair). He brought religious, political and gender issues into a framework of love, friendship and maternal feelings.

In 1911 Tagore composed the song `*Jana-gana-mana-adhinayaka*' which was sung at the Calcutta Session of the Indian National Congress, 1911 and which is now the national anthem of India. In 1912 he went abroad and translations (many of them done by himself) of his poems caught the attention of the Western world. It recognized his genius in 1913 with the Nobel Prize for his *Gitanjali* (Song-offering), a collection of short poems with spiritual messages.

Tagore used the prize money entirely on developing his educational project at Santiniketan. In 1918, it was made an university named Visva Bharati, with the ideal of international peace and harmony. The years 1914-17 saw many short stories (later brought together in *Galpaguchha*, A Bunch of Stories) which were then a relatively new form in Bengali literature.

In 1915, the British government conferred a Knighthood upon Tagore. He could now be called `Sir Rabindranath'.

In 1916 Tagore wrote the novel *GhareBaire* (Within and Without the Home) where he wrote against the mindless boycott of British goods as a tool for displaying nationalism.

But in 1918 came the Jallianwalla Bagh massacre. Tagore's spirited protest was by way of returning the Knighthood.

From a distance, Tagore had developed an association with Gandhiji. It was Tagore who had given him the epithet of `Mahatma'. The Tagore song `*Ekla chalo* (Go it alone)' was one of Gandhi ji's favourites. With Jawaharlal Nehru too Rabindranath had a fond association. For a short while, Indira Gandhi (then Nehru) too stayed and studied at Santiniketan.

Tagore grew old but he continued to be prolific in almost every form of creative writing. He had his critics and sometimes felt hurt at their criticism. But the accolades that he got were overwhelming. He stood head and shoulders above any other contemporary writer, including Sharatchandra Chattopadhyaya who was himself an admirer of Tagore. The songs written (and sometimes tuned) by him became a new genre known as *Rabindra-sangeet.* They are usually based on Indian *ragas* but some are in the Baul tradition and some are even set to Western tunes.

Till the end, Tagore remained completely dedicated to the development of Visva Bharati and the adjoining areas. It became a centre which attracted many artists and intellectuals, Indian and international. For funding, he went on world tours with a troupe of Santiniketan students. He took up painting and developed a most original style which won the appreciation of the Western critics. Tagore was a multi-faceted genius. Poet, playwright, story-writer, novelist, essayist, artist, educationist, patriot... he had many dimensions. He wrote for adults as well as children. Young and old, men and women, all admired his work.

People began to refer to him as *Kavi-guru* (Master of Poets) and *Guru-deva* (God among Preceptors).

He had always been handsome and now, with long silver hair and beard, slightly bent, dressed in loose, dark robes, he had a saintly appearance. Tagore was an affectionate father and uncle, although he lost several of his children, nephews and nieces. Above all superstition, he had wedded his only surviving son to a child-widow and was very attached to his daughter-in-law. Although he had no direct grandchild, he was most loving to his adoptive grandchildren and grand-nieces-and-nephews.

In 1941, reluctantly, he came from Santiniketan to Kolkata to be treated for kidney problems. But he never recovered from the surgery and passed away on 7 August 1941 (`*Baishey Shravan*').

People poured into the streets of Kolkata to join the procession to his cremation. To date, Tagore-lovers observe *Baishe Shravan* with songs and prayers.

Many of Tagore's works have been made into films by acclaimed film-directors like Nitin Bose, Satyajit Ray, Tapan Sinha and Rituparno Ghosh. Translations have made Tagore popular than ever in the global era. In fact, Tagore was an emissary of 'globalization' more than a century before it occurred in the world. Visva Bharati (now a central university with UGC funding) has as its motto: *Yatra visva bhavati ekaneedam* (Where the world becomes a single nest).

Rabindranath Tagore will be ever-relevant, ever-revered.

❐

On the Stories

In this book we offer you selected stories from Tagore's famous short-story-collection *Galpaguchha* (Bunch of Stories).Even today they impress readers with their astuteness of observation, depth of understanding, warmth of feelings and beauty of expression. Each story has a relevance that transcends time and space. A few have a subtle humour, a few are chilling. They display a wide variety of themes and characters, a deep love of nature and a philosophy of rising above material possessions. Tagore valued freedom of thought and several of his stories show how crushing traditional schooling can be. He also urged the need for educating the girl-child and giving her a good chance in life. While he wrote against the persistence of superstitions, he also believed in the supernatural, sometimes even using the planchet to call up spirits of the many who had departed from his life.

It is with these considerations in mind that we have selected the stories for this collection.

Samapti- **The Completion** is a charming romance with a subtle lesson. Village girl Mrimoyee is a tomboy not yet ready for love and marriage. Apurva, a young law-student of Kolkata, falls in love with her and marries her against his mother's wishes. But Mrinmoyee is too much of a child to respond. Hurt though he is, her husband does not force or pressurize her. He just leaves for Kolkata. Left to herself, Mrinmoyee grows up and matures into a woman and wife. She visits Kolkata and her husband's love meets its completion. This is not just a pleasant love story but one that emphasizes freedom and individual growth. It is part of the famous Bengali film *Teen Kanya* directed by Satyajit

Ray in 1961.The Hindi film *Abodh* (1984, directed by Hiren Nag) is also based on it.

***Chhuti*- Holidays** is a heart-rending tale. Even if it is for educational opportunities, exile from familiar surroundings and home life can create devastating pressure on the adolescent. High-spirited village lad Phatik is sent off to Kolkata to get better education and ease the pressure on his widowed mother. But homesickness and alien surroundings bring his life to an untimely end.

In ***Chitrakar*- The Painter**, fatherless Chunilal wants to scribble and paint but his worldly-wise uncle comes down very strictly upon his artistic attempts. Chuni's mother, in spite of being a helpless young widow, rebels against her brother and saves the artist in her child.

***Khata*- The Exercise Book** depicts the deprivation of the girl child. Child marriage not only prevents Uma from receiving education but tortures her for her attempts at self-expression. In spite of the recent drive for the education of the girl child, Umas can still be found in Indian households.

***Megh O Roudra*- Clouds and Sunshine**- Tears and laughter, joy and sorrow...alternate in life. Their shifting pattern is woven into the story of little Giribala and her young tutor-cum-friend Shashishekhar. Underneath the childhood romance there is depiction of gender bias and contemporary political struggle.

In **The Postmaster,** a young man from Kolkata is posted to a rural area and finds life dull and boring. Orphaned girl-child Ratan draws water for him and cooks for him. The postmaster occupies his leisure in teaching her how to read and write. This creates in Ratan a desire for self-improvement as well as an affection for her teacher and employer. The postmaster falls ill and she nurses him devotedly. But he seeks and gets a transfer and Ratan feels abandoned. This too is part of the Ray film Teen Kanya (1961).

Several kids have talent but do not conform to set patterns of behaviour. They have a restlessness in them that parents and guardians find baffling. They are never at rest and often rejected by family and society. ***Aapad*- The Troubles** and ***Atithi*-The Guest** are about such 'difficult' children, much misunderstood even now despite the advances in child psychology. *Atithi* had been filmed in 1969 by director Tappan Sinhala.

Far ahead of the Chipko Movement, Tagore had written about conservation of plants and the intimate connection between man and Nature. In **Balai-The Boy and the Tree**,

Balai is a gentle, imaginative child who feels one with Nature. He develops an attachment to a plant and does not let his uncle axe it down. But in his absence the deed gets done and his childless aunt takes long to forgive her husband for it.

In ***Subha*- Eloquent,** the girl named Subha has a similar bonding with Nature. Because she has a speech disability, human beings do not understand her and reject her cruelly. The story underscores the helplessness of the disabled. Although the times are changing, there is still need for sensitization on the issue of physical challenges. In 1964 it had been made into a film directed by Partha Pratim Chowdhury.

***Pan-raksha*- Keeping a Promise** is the moving story of a poor weaver's lifelong sacrifice for his kid brother who is somewhat wayward. By the time Rashik becomes a mature man, his brother has worn himself out and died, keeping his promise or vow of getting Rashik a bicycle.

The faithful man-servants of yesteryears are now impossible to find. Often it was not just feudal obligations but genuine attachment that bound them to their masters. In ***Khokababur***

***Pratyavartan*- The Young Master's Return**, Tagore shows how dedicated an old servant can be to the child of the family he works for.

To atone for a moment's mistake, Raicharan makes a personal sacrifice that is rare and heart-rending. Tagore's childhood at Jorasanko had been spent under a regime of faithful family servants. In his own *zamindari* days too he had come across common folk with tremendous dedication to their master.

People of all countries and cultures have certain feelings in common. A father feels the same way about his daughter whether he is from Bengal or Kabul. In ***Kabuliwala,*** probably the most famous of Tagore's stories, we find the assertion of faith in the universal character of humanity. It was made into a Bengali film in 1957 under the direction of Tapan Sinha and a Hindi film in 1961 under the direction of Hemen Gupta.

In ***Ichchapuran*- Wish-Fulfillment,** Tagore touches lightly upon the issue of youth and old age. The child envies the power the adult seemingly has over him. The old man envies the agile and carefree child. But if they exchange places, the result is not enviable either. *Icchapuran* is a fun story with a serious lesson.

***Master-mashai*- The Tutor** is a tragic story about the fate of a poor young man who is too fond of his wayward pupil Benu. Their teacher-student relationship transcends the usual forms and ends in a tragic death, and a haunting ghost story.

***Moni-hara*– Robbed of the Gem** is a chilling account of how terrible attachment to material possessions can be. Childless Moni (which means `gem' or `jewel')is over-attached to her jewellery. Her husband Phanibhushan adores her but when he needs her jewellery (his own gifts to her) to help him out of debts, she makes off with them rather than help him out. On the way she is robbed and killed and comes back to haunt her poor sorrowing husband.

Moni-hara is part of Teen Kanya (1961).

***Guptadhan*- Hidden Treasure** is not just a simple story of treasure hunt. Mrityunjaya gives up half his life decoding a set of clues that will enable him to find hidden treasure that supposedly belongs to his family. But once he does come upon the treasure in a deep well within the forest, he realizes that there are more valuable things in life like open air and nature .This is a story with a message of relinquishment, of the conquest of covetousness.

***Sampatti- samarpan*- Bequeathing the Property**

Sampatti-samarpan is a starker story. In ancient India, there was the bizarre custom of appointing a *yaksha,* a spirit, as the trustee or guardian of wealth being left to absent or untraceable descendants. The wealth or treasure was buried underground and some youth was buried along with it. The youth would starve or suffocate to death, and people would imagine him to have become a *yaksha*. Here a miserly grandfather unknowingly kills his own heir - his own grandson.

Being the grandson of `Prince' Dwarakanath and the son of 'Maharshi' Devendranath, here (as in *Monihara* and *Guptadhan*), Rabindranath Tagore shows what most macabre consequences material attachment can have.

With this rationale for the selection of our stories, we invite the readers to the stories themselves.

Dipavali Sen

Dipavali Sen is an academic, formerly of Visva Bharati University, and has published work on Tagore in magazines as well as a British Council collection.

❐

1

The Completion

Samapti

1

After graduating from Kolkata, Apurva-krishna was returning to his riverside village.

The skies had cleared after a few days of downpour and the river, through which the boat was passing, was narrow, but filled to the brim, As it was a surprise visit, there was no one to receive him at the *ghat* (embankment).As soon as the boat reached the *ghat,* a happy Apurva hurriedly got off the boat with his luggage and as he did so, he lost his balance and fell right into the muddy patch on the river bank. Before he could recover, he heard ripples of loud laughter. Embarrassed, he turned around to find a girl sitting on a heap of bricks on the bank. She was in splits.

Apurva immediately recognized her as Mrinmoyee, their neighbour's daughter. Earlier they had settled further down the river but due to soil erosion, had come and re-settled in their village. She was a tomboy, who played only with the boys. While the village folk endearingly called her `*paglee'* (madcap), the womenfolk were quite terrified by her.

She was dark, with short, curly hair half-way down her back. Her face had a boyish look while her dark eyes had no look of shyness, fear or inhibition. She was tall and healthy, but because of her childlike ways, the village folks did not bother to figure out if she was old enough to get married. If they had, they would have been critical of her parents.

Apurva managed to get up from the muddy patch and hurriedly made his way home. But he could not get away from the image of the young girl sitting on the brick mound and giggling away.

2

Apurva's mother was very happy with this pleasant surprise and after showering all her affection on the son, and giving him a scrumptious meal, she got down to her favourite topic, that of getting him married off. Apurva had always made the excuse that he would not marry till he had become a graduate but now that the excuse was no longer valid, he thought he would buy time by actually wanting to meet the girl. This was naturally considered offensive, but his mother agreed. Accordingly, a prospective candidate was short listed and one evening Apurva, dressed in the finest aristocratic attire, complete with a silk umbrella and a pair of polished shoes, went over to see her.

The over-dressed girl looked more like a bundle of clothes. Apurva enquired about her education level and the girl was too shy to answer. In the midst of all this, suddenly there was a commotion outside. Mrinmoyee stormed in to the room, slapped the girl's brother on his back, took a look around, went up to the girl and pulled down the sari from over her head and ran out with a mischievous laugh. As she was accepted to be a tomboy, no one said anything. As Apurva was leaving, he found his well-polished pair of shoes missing! As he walked home in a borrowed pair of old slippers, suddenly he was greeted by laughter spurting out from behind the wayside trees. It was Mrinmoyee, unable to hold back her amusement to see Apurva wearing the ill fitting chappals, that too with a dress which called for shoes. A puzzled Apurva kept looking here and there when, still laughing, she suddenly emerged from the trees with the pair of missing shoes. She kept them in front of Apurva and was trying to run away when Apurva got hold of her by the arms.

She tried to twist her arms and free herself, but could not. The sunlight fell on her face with curly hair all across it. Apurva kept hold of her and looked deep into her eyes. He kept looking, and then let her off.

If Apurva had beaten her up, Mrinmoyee would have understood. But she could not make any sense of the subtle and silent punishment he gave her.

She ran off and her laughter echoed all over the place. Apurva returned home with very slow steps.

3

"How did you find the girl?" Apurva's mother asked with an air of expectation.

"Oh, I liked one of them," Apurva replied.

"Why, how many girls did you see!" his mother was surprised.

After some hesitation, Apurva admitted that he had chosen Mrinmoyee over the girl he had actually gone to see and that he was going to marry none other than her. Shocked at her son's taste, Apurva's mother objected for a few days, and then gave in to her son's wishes. The village folk were fond of Mrinmoyee but no one had thought of her as appropriate for a daughter-in-law. Now everybody got down to the task of grooming Mrinmoyee for the marriage. Her mother and all the elder ladies took turns to advise her on the process of marriage and the duties of a wife. Mrinmoyee realized that marriage was going to be a hindrance to her freedom and stubbornly declared that she was not going to get married.

4

The marriage however did take place.

Mrinmoyee's father was a clerk in a steamboat company. He was posted in a small station further down the river, weighing luggage and selling tickets. He did not get the leave to come and attend the wedding.

Once the wedding was over, Mrinmoyee's entire world shrunk into the household of Apurva's mother. With a very stern face, she made it clear to Mrinmoyee that, now that she was married, she had to mend her ways. This irked Mrinmoyee and one afternoon she ran away from the house. The whole village searched for her and she was found sitting in a discarded chariot of the village deity that was lying there under a Banyan tree. Needless to say, she was rebuked by her mother, mother in law and all other womenfolk of the village.

That night Apurva went up to Mrinmoyee and asked her if she loved him.

"No", replied Mrinmoyee with spirit. "I will never love you."

"Why, what wrong have I done?" Apurva asked.

"Why did you marry me?" Mrinmoyee spewed out her anger at him.

Seeing the daughter in law's rebellious nature, Apurva's mother decided to lock her up in the room the next day. Mrinmoyee was like a caged bird flapping its wings all over the cage, looking for an escape route. She tore up the quilt and lay on the floor crying for her father.

Apurva tried to cheer her up by quietly opening the door of the room and telling her that he had sneaked in Rakhal, a playmate, to come and play with her. She refused to play and, seeing her temper, Rakhal ran away.

The next day Mrinmoyee received a letter from her father blessing the newly married couple and regretting the fact that he could not be present for the ceremony.

"I will go to my father", Mrinmoyee went up to her mother-in-law and said.

"What an absurd idea!" scolded her mother-in-law. "One doesn't even know properly where your father works!"

Locking herself up in her room, Mrinmoyee wept and prayed. "Baba, come and take me away. I don't have anyone here. I will die if I stay here."

In the thick of night, when Apurva was asleep, Mrinmoyee quietly opened the door of her room and left the house. She knew the lay of the land well but did not know the way that led to her father's place. Her belief was that the route taken by the postman, known those days as the Runner, could take you to any destination you desired. She walked almost all night through the jungle and at the end of the road, near the river bank, she found a Runner.

"Take me to my father at Kushiganj", Mrinmoyee appealed to him. But the Runner had no idea as to where Kushiganj was. As the day dawned, the riverside came to life with people going to the market. Mrinmoyee called out to a boatman to row her to Kushiganj. From the next boat, a man offered to take her there. This was their village boatman and he knew all about Mrinmoyee and her ways. As the boat rolled from side to side, a tired Mrinmoyee fell asleep. When she woke up, she found herself on her bed in her own room.

Her mother-in-law not only said harsh things to her but also made slighting references to her father.

"Ma," Apurva said shyly, "What's wrong in sending *bou* (the bride) off for a couple of days to see her father?"

This infuriated his mother even more.

5

But that night Apurva woke her up and offered to take her to her father. Mrinmoyee was so happy that she caught hold of Apurva's hand. Thrilled with her touch, Apurva took her out of the house and on a boat journey to her father's workplace at Kushiganj. All day the boat sailed along the river and a happy Mrinmoyee kept asking Apurva about the various places they passed, which were all new to her. After a most enjoyable journey, they reached Kushiganj.

Her father was suitably surprised and happy at the sudden arrival of the daughter and son in law and the next few days were happy days of reunion with all three trying their hand in culinary delights, mostly with disastrous results. After a few days it was time to return home.

6

Apurva had left a note for her mother explaining where they were going. So she had not been worried. But she was severely offended and hardly spoke to the young couple on their return. The atmosphere of the house became heavy with her silent disfavour. When it became intolerable, Apurva went up to his mother and said, "Ma, I have to return to Kolkata to study Law".

" Take your wife to Kolkata with you", she said stiffly. But the night before leaving Apurva found Mrinmoyee in tears. "Aren't you happy about coming to Kolkata with me?" he asked her.

"No", replied Mrinmoyee. "I want to go and stay with my mother."

"So be it. But remember, till I get a letter from you, I will not return".

Mrinmoyee fell asleep but Apurva stayed up gazing at her sleeping, so innocent and unconscious of her own womanhood.

Just before he left, Apurva asked Mrinmoyee for a kiss.

"Will you kiss me just once, out of your own free will, out of love?" He looked so serious and the request seemed so strange to her that Mrinmoyee burst into peals of laughter. She did try to kiss Apurva, but every time she tried, she broke out laughing. After a while, Apurva gave up and jokingly boxed Mrinmoyee's ears.

Reaching her to her mother's hut in the same village, Apurva took leave of his mother. Both were deeply hurt but silent.

7

Mrinmoyee returned to her mother's house. But soon she found out that nothing seemed interesting any more. She felt that her whole world had changed. She did not know what to do with her time. The entire village suddenly felt empty.

She could not understand why she wanted to go to Kolkata so badly now, when only the other night she had felt no such desire.

Everything had lost its taste for her.

Her childhood had dropped off from her - like a dried-up leaf from its stalk.

An invisible sword had sliced through her childhood and youth. It had happened some time back, without her knowing it, and the pieces were still holding together. But now, something had given it a shake, and the childhood had fallen off from her.

The old hut and the old bed no longer felt like her own. She now wanted another house, another room, another bed.

The village folk no longer saw her playing with the boys. No longer did her laughter ring out. Rather then play with her, Rakhal got scared to see her now. "Take me to my in-laws' place", she told her mother.

Apurva's mother pressed Mrinmoyee to her bosom as she fell at her feet. She had been remembering how Apurva had gone away, hurt at her unwillingness to let Mrinmoyee stay with her.

No words were spoken, but Mrinmoyee and her mother-in-law developed a perfect understanding.

Time went by. Apurva stayed on at Kolkata. Mrinmoyee thought of the kiss he had asked for and regretted her own childish behaviour with Apurva.

Apurva had said that till she wrote to him she would not come back to the village. Mrinmoyee made an effort to write him a letter. In crooked letters she wrote out:

How are you? Come home.

On the envelope she simply wrote:

Srijukta Babu Apurvakrishna Roy.

She got a trusted maid to drop the letter, but a letter without an address reaches nowhere. Nor did Apurva come home.

8

Apurva's mother felt that it was she who her son was angry with. "It's been a long time since he left for Kolkata", she said to Mrinmoyee. "I think we should make a trip to Kolkata. Do you wish to come with me?"

Mrinmoyee immediately agreed and unannounced, the two ladies landed up at Kolkata .

They stayed at the house of Apurva's married sister.

Her husband informed Apurva that his mother had reached Kolkata and that Apurva should join them for dinner.

Apurva rushed to his sister's house and asked his mother if all was well.

"Yes, everything is fine. Since you did not come for your vacations, I have come to take you back to the village."

Apurva's sister asked him why he did not get his wife over to Kolkata. Apurva cited the Law examination as an excuse. In spite of good food and cheery jokes from his hosts, his heart was heavy. His mother had taken the trouble of coming all the way, he thought; couldn't his wife have come as well? As he had not received any letters from Mrinmoyee, he had no idea of the change in her, and thought that she must have refused to come, even if his mother had asked her to do so. But he felt shy to directly ask his mother about Mrinmoyee. Dinner over, there rose a storm.

His hosts requested Apurva to stay back for the night and escorted him to a room which had no lights. His sister offered to get a light but Apurva politely refused. As soon as his sister left the room, he groped towards the bed. Just then, with a tinkle of bangles, two soft arms clasped him in a tight embrace and two soft lips rained kisses upon him – kisses wet with tears.

Apurva gave a start and then realized that what had remained incomplete in laughter had now found its completion in tears.

❐

2

Holidays

Chhuti

Phatik Chakraborti was the leader of the young boys in the village. They were playing by the side of the river. Phatik suddenly had the bright idea of rolling away a log that had been lying on the river-bank to be made into the mast of the ship. All the boys agreed wholeheartedly, tickled at the vision of the owner shocked to see the log gone when he required it. Just as every body had got ready to push the log, Makhan, Phatik's younger brother, came up and took his seat upon the log. He looked very thoughtful and sedate.

One of the boys tried to make him move. Makhan did not budge.

"Move or I shall beat you up," Phatik threatened his brother. This merely made Makhan settle down even more comfortably on the log. Losing face before his followers, Phatik felt like delivering a tight slap to his kid brother. But then, he had another idea. Why not roll the log with Makhan sitting on it?

The boys under Phatik's command began to push together. Makhan, for a moment felt as if this was an honour of some sort to be pushed along. But none among them had realized the danger of this activity. By the time the log had made one turn, Makhan had rolled off it, and fallen down. This unexpected success of the game instantly cheered the gang up. But Makhan, humiliated and hurt, jumped up from the ground and fell upon his elder brother. He hit Phatik blindly and clawed his face. Then, wailing loudly, he left for home.

The game was over for the other kids as well. Phatik plucked out some wild grass and chewed them, sitting on a half-sunk boat on the river-bank. A little later a boat arrived and anchored there. A middle-aged gentleman, sporting a salt and pepper moustache and grey hair, got down. He asked Phatik the way to the Chakraborti home.

Phatik casually replied, "There", and actually pointed to almost nowhere.

"Where exactly? Which way?" the elderly gentleman asked. "I don't know", Phatik showed no interest (even though the Chakraborti home meant his own!)The visitor had to ask his way from some other people. Shortly his mother sent someone to fetch Phatik home.

"I am not coming home," said Phatik whereupon the man just lifted him up and carried him home. His furious mother charged Phatik with beating up his brother - again.

"I did not beat him up," said Phatik. "Ask Makhan".

But Makhan said that he had indeed been beaten up by Phatik. This enraged Phatik who dealt Makhan a slap. "Lying again!" he accused Makhan.

Their mother took the younger child's side and rained a few blows upon Phatik. Phatik gave her a push.

"How dare you raise your hands upon me?" cried his mother.

Just then the gentleman who had just arrived in the village made his way in. "What is the happening here?" he exclaimed.

"Dada, it is you! I don't believe it!" The mother was full of joy and surprise

It turned out that the gentleman who had asked for directions was Phatik's mother's brother, that is, Mama or maternal uncle to Phatik and Makhan. His name was Bishwambhar.

He had left home years ago to seek his fortune outside Bengal and had returned after years. During the time he was absent, the sister had got married, become a mother of two and even been widowed.

The next few days were spent in entertaining Bishwambhar. While leaving, Bishwambhar asked his sister about the education and personality development of her sons.

"Phatik is never in any mood to study and is thoroughly undisciplined, while Makhan, the other one, is well mannered, studious and has a pleasant temperament," his widowed sister explained.

On hearing this Bishwambhar offered to take Phatik with him to Kolkata and bring him up, fund his schooling and his grooming. The widow agreed.

"What do you say, Phatik? " Bishwambhar turned to Phatik. "Will you come with this Mama of yours to Kolkata?"

Phatik jumped up and said "Yes!"

His mother felt a bit hurt at his enthusiasm to leave, although she also felt a little relieved. She had always been scared of Phatik beating up Makhan or doing some harm to him.

Phatik was so thrilled at this prospect of going to Kolkata that, on the eve of his departure, he gifted his fishing rod and kite-flying equipments to Makhan, adding that Makhan could, in turn, bequeath them to his sons and grandsons!

Reaching his uncle's home in Kolkata he was introduced to his Mami or aunt. But she was in no way favourably disposed to the idea of Phatik coming and staying with them. She already had three kids to look after and the entry of an unknown, ill-mannered and ill-educated village-lad did not meet with her approval.

Phatik was at the age of transformation from the child to the adolescent. As a youth of thirteen or fourteen years, he did not rouse affection in people. His voice lost the sweetness of childhood and he outgrew his clothes pretty fast. He was quite ill-at-ease at this stage of life and felt awkward and embarrassed before the entire world. Yet this was the time when he developed an extra need for affection from people. An alien household seemed hell to him. He longed to be with his mother and harshness from women in general seemed intolerable.

His Mami was not at all fond of Phatik and this hurt him no end. Whenever his Mami wanted him to run errands, he would do it with such excessive joy that he would overdo it. His Mami would then dampen all his enthusiasm by telling him to cut it short and go away and study. This, Phatik found to be most cruel.

Apart from this lack of affection, there was the restriction that the city walls put upon him.

He yearned for the free and easy days in the village, the fields, the river, the village lads and even the mother who had been unfair to him at times.A dumb, animal-like love for her tormented this lanky, gawky youth – so nervous and embarrassed under his uncle's roof. He took no interest in studies and became unmindful and disinterested. When the school-teacher beat him up, he took the punishment with a dull silence.

One day he gathered up courage to ask his uncle, "Mama, when will I go home to my mother?"

"Let the schools close for Puja holidays," was the reply.

The Puja holidays were in autumn. That was far away!

One day Phatik lost his textbook. As it is, he did not learn his lessons well. Now with the loss of the book, his performance was so bad that his teacher began to beat him up every day. His position in the school became so humiliating that even his cousins joined the other students in making fun of him.

Phatik could not take it any more and, shamefacedly confessed to his aunt that he had lost his book. With lines of irritation on her face, Mami refused to buy him a new book. Phatik came away silently, feeling very low that he was wasting money that belonged to a family that was not his. He felt a grudge against his mother for sending him there.

That night Phatik started getting a headache followed by fever. He knew if he announced himself sick, his aunt would see it as an additional inconvenience. He felt in his bones how she would jibe at his falling ill. He felt ashamed to ask for care from anyone other than his mother.

Next morning, he went missing. Search in the neighbourhood proved futile. A drizzle which had started at night turned into incessant rain and people searching for Phatik got wet and inconvenienced. Finally Bishwambhar informed the police. The downpour continued and at night; when the water on the streets was almost knee-deep, a police vehicle brought Phatik back to Bishwambhar's house. He was muddied and drenched, shivering and red-eyed. Bishwambhar had to carry him to his room.

His wife had also been anxious and irritable all day. Now she spoke out:

"Why take all this trouble for a boy who is not our own. Send him home!" Phatik burst out crying, "I was going to my mother. They brought me back!"

His fever rose even higher and the whole night he was in delirium. A doctor was summoned. Phatik managed to open his bloodshot eyes and glance stupidly at the ceiling. "Mama", he asked Bishwambhar, "Are the holidays here?"

His uncle wiped his tears and came and sat beside him, holding his thin, hot hands. Phatik again began to mutter in his fever: "Don't beat me, Ma. Believe me, I have done no wrong!"

Next day, he became conscious for a while and looked around the room - as if expecting somebody. Disappointed, he turned on his side again, with his face to the wall.

"I have sent for your mother, Phatik", Bishwambhar whispered in his ear. Another day passed. The doctor declared that Phatik's condition was getting critical.

In the dimly-lit room, Bishwambhar waited by his nephew's bedside - hoping every moment for his sister's arrival. Phatik continued to be in delirium.

Some time later, his mother, who had been brought over to Kolkata, rushed in to see Phatik.

"Phatik, my precious!" she wailed as she fell upon his bed.

"Yes, Ma?" Phatik answered, as though very naturally.

"O Phatik, my child!" the mother called out again.

Phatik turned over, and without addressing anyone in particular, said very softly, "Ma, my holidays are here, and Ma, I am going home."

❐

3

The Painter

Chitrakar

Chunilal was four years old. Young as he was, he had lost his father, an established lawyer named Mukunda. With his widowed mother Satyavati, he lived under the guardianship of his father's brother, named Gobinda. Brothers Gobinda and Mukunda had come to Kolkata early in their lives. That is where Mukunda had his legal practice and Gobinda pursued his trade – which was money-making.

Right from the time he had come to the city, Gobinda had dedicated his life to accumulating wealth .He referred to it as simply `paisa-kara'. Through narrow and often crooked ways, Gobinda proceeded towards his goal. He now had a high position in a British firm trading in gunny bags.

Mukunda had also established his repute as a lawyer, and even bought a house in Kolkata. But he died suddenly, leaving not merely the property he had acquired but also some debts. To survive, his bereaved family had to lead a very frugal life. His wife needed to be most economical. Little Chunilal could hardly have the life the neighbourhood children were enjoying.

According to Mukunda's will, the entire responsibility of his family would be Gobinda's. His wife Satyavati and son Chunilal would be under Gobinda's guardianship.

"*Paisa karo* - make money", Gobinda chanted into Chunilal's ear. Money-making was over and above everything.

From the very first day of his guardianship, uncle Gobinda made this clear to his wards, Chunilal as well as his mother Satyavati. But Satyavati was against the initiation of her son, as if by a guru, into the worship of wealth. She did not say anything outright but her very behaviour obstructed the path Gobinda wanted Chunilal to follow.

Satyavati, right from her childhood, had a great interest in artwork. It was her hobby to fashion craft items out of clay, flour, paper, or cloth. Pressing the juice out of flowers and leaves, she made paint and dye for herself, and used them to add colour to the odds and ends she made. Her passion was for making objects of art - not objects of utility. The items she crafted out had hardly any practical purpose. Often they were new and strange, and useless. In the everyday world, they had no meaning or worth. Sometimes they brought criticism or ridicule upon Satyavati. For instance, there would be important visits to make to close relatives, but Satyavati would forget and be lost in her craftwork in her own room- may be pressing lumps of clay into fancy shapes.

But Mukunda, her husband, regarded all this with affection and amusement. He did not regard his wife's handiwork as worthy of the exalted name of art. But he felt gently amused at the fact that his wife wasted a lot of her time in such unnecessary and useless activities. If anyone else in the household commented on it, Mukunda always spoke out in favour of his wife. Sometimes on his way back from the court, he used to buy some art material for his wife—paint, pencils, and colourful silk pieces. He would quietly arrange his gifts in Satyavati's bedroom, and give her a surprise. He could not tell the difference between the portrait of a man and the sketch of a bird. But he would often praise his "Satu" for her work, and provide her with patient patronage.

Satyavati knew how lucky she was to have such a husband, but she lost that good fortune with his death.

To be an artist one needs certain materials. Earlier Satyavati had got them without asking and never felt them to be favours. But now she felt most embarrassed to ask for them. She began to cut down on her own food expenses, bought her art material in secrecy, and worked behind closed doors. She was not scared of Gobinda's scolding but she did not want his insensitive glances upon her small and strange creations.

Chunilal at first just watched and assisted his mother my reaching out paint or paper to her as and when necessary. But soon, through this process of co-operation, he too developed a tremendous fancy for such art and craft work. It became an addiction and because he was a four-year-old child, it did not remain a secret or hidden. It spilled out of his exercise books and expressed itself on the walls. Even Chuni's clothes and face and hands began to give away that he was going after arts and crafts rather than money-making. His uncle observed it and began to make him suffer for it.

But just as Gobinda became stricter towards his ward and nephew, Satyavati became more and more encouraging. She began to assist him in what to Mukunda was a criminal waste of time and energy. Whenever Mukunda went out of Kolkata with his boss, mother and son tasted a great sense of freedom and indulged in their labour of love with abandon. For instance, they would fashion strange animals out of clay - half-dog half-cat - creations of fantasy. Then they would press them back into lumps of clay again - or destroy them - so that there was nothing to give them away when their guardian came back.

Satyavati's family had a natural inclination towards arts and crafts. Artistic tendencies ran in the family blood. An older cousin named Rangalal suddenly came into a lot of fame at this juncture. His paintings were not true to life. Even his imagination was off-beat. Some people ridiculed his bizarre style and defective technique. Others hailed them as modern art. Rangalal was much-criticized as well as much-acclaimed.

Once when Gobinda happened to be out of town, Rangalal came to look Satyavati up. He had to thump on the door loudly before he could gain entry. For Satyavati and Chunilal had shut themselves up and become happily and completely engrossed in their work.

Rangalal found it difficult even to take his steps. The floor was full of sheets and even scraps of paper and cloth. There were drawings and paintings scattered all around. He glanced at them and was most impressed by the natural and free way in which Chunilal had expressed his impressions of the world around him, creating his own creatures of strange shapes and colours. "They are so fresh and original" exclaimed Rangalal. "Show me the all the rest."

But where would they find the other pictures and items of their creation? They had destroyed them all for fear of Gobinda.

"From now on, whatever you paint or make, I will come and collect", said Rangalal. "Promise me never to destroy them."

Another day, with Gobinda not yet back, Satyavati and Chunilal were at it again. From the morning it had been raining and the grey skies did not reveal how late in the day it was getting to be.

Chuni-babu was drawing boats sailing in the river. The wild waves were trying to swallow up boats (that did not look like boats) and the drawing sheets were a welter of paint, water and colour.

So engrossed Chuni was in his world, that he had not noticed that he had left the door open. Gobinda came by. He took one look and roared out, "What's all this?"

Chuni trembled and grew pale.

Mukunda knew at once that this was the reason Chuni could not remember his history dates.

Meanwhile, Chuni tried to hide his picture inside his clothes and appeared even guiltier.

Gobinda snatched the picture away from him and looked at it. What he saw made him all the more astonished. What on earth was this stuff? Wrong history dates seemed to be better than the strange pictures Chuni had drawn.

Mukunda tore up the picture into shreds. Chuni gave a loud sob.

From the *puja* room Satyavati heard him. She saw the torn pieces of Chuni's picture lying on the floor. She saw Chuni lying on the floor among them.

Till now Satyavati had never protested against anything that her brother-in-law and guardian had said or done. She had silently borne everything since it was upon Gobinda that her husband had reposed his trust. But now she spoke out – in a voice a-tremble with anger and wet with tears. :"Why did you tear up Chuni's painting?"

"Doesn't he have to study?" asked Gobinda. "What will

happen to him in the future?"

"Even if he becomes a beggar in the future", answered Satyavati, "let him not become like you. God has given him an asset. Let it shine brighter than any money you can make. As a mother, this is how I bless him."

"I cannot let go of my responsibility", replied Gobinda, "Tomorrow itself I will send him off to a boarding school. You will otherwise ruin his future."

Gobinda went off to his office. It began to rain heavily. The streets of Kolkata started to get water-logged. Satyavati gripped Chuni's hand. "Come, let's go"

"Where to, Ma?" Chuni asked.

"Let's go away from here".

Satyavati found her way to Rangalal's house. Wading through the waters to get to the front door, she entered the house, holding Chunilal's hand. "You be his guardian", she said to Rangalal. "Save Chuni from the pursuit of money-making."

❐

4

The Exercise Book

Khata

Ever since she has learnt to write, Uma has become a pest. On the walls of every room in the house, she has written in big, unformed letters: *jal parey pata narey* (raindrops fall and the leaves move).

Her sister-in-law was reading a mystery story, and had kept it under her pillow. Uma hunted it out and scrawled all over it with pencil: *kalo jaw, lal phul* (black water, red flower). She had almost obliterated the fine print of the horoscope book the family constantly referred to, in large letters. Right in the middle of her father's housekeeping accounts, she had written: *lekhapara karey jei garighora charey shei* (It is the one who studies who gets to ride in cars).

Uma's elder brother Gobindolal, though not a great intellectual, often wrote popular pieces for magazines. He had put in a lot of effort in one and got it printed, but Uma scribbled all over it with big black letters: *Gopal baro bhalo chheleye* (Gopal is a very good boy). Gobindolal was furious. He beat his little sister up and took away whatever meager writing material she had (such as, a pencil stub, a blunt and ink-stained pen).The humiliated girl could not fully comprehend why she was being so severely punished. She sat in a corner and cried.

After a while, her elder brother felt a little sorry – and made up with Uma by giving her writing materials back to her, along with a whole new exercise book, lined and bound.

Uma was then seven years old. Ever since then the exercise book became her constant companion. It reposed in her arms all through the day and in the night, under her pillow.

Uma went to the girls' school in the village, escorted by the maid. The exercise book accompanied her, causing surprise and envy among her classmates. In the first year she took down short rhymes in it. She used to sit on the bedroom floor, clutch her copy, and loudly sing out what she had noted down. In the second year, she began to jot down lines of her own. For example, just below a fable she had copied down, she had written: I love Jashi a lot.

No, no, this is not a love story. Jashi is not some village lad but the maid who has been working for the household for ages. But some days later, completely opposite sentiments regarding Jashi were found recorded.

Again, there was the line: I will never speak to Hari (not Haricharan but Haridasi). But a few pages later, there were lines saying that Hari was her best friend in the world.

At the age of nine, Uma was married off to a young man who was a friend of Gobindolal, and like him, also wrote for the newspapers. He was conservative in his outlook, and the entire neighbourhood praised him for his loyalty to traditions.

While sending her off, the mother asked her to obey her mother-in-law and do household work rather than remain engrossed in her reading and writing.

"Don't scribble on the walls there", his elder brother warned her. "It is not that kind of a household. And never ever scrawl over any piece that Peareymohan writes."

Uma felt quite scared. Jashi accompanied her to the in-laws' place. With affectionate consideration, she took Uma's exercise book along. It was a part of her parental place, a history of her short stay under care of her parents - a history written in crooked, unformed letters, a sweet taste of independence in her untimely entry into the prison of household duties.

Once Jashi went back, Uma took out her exercise book from the tin trunk she had. Her tears falling, she wrote: Jashi has gone home. I will go home to my mother." Soon after there was another entry: "If my elder brother once takes me home, I will never again spoil his writings."

Uma's father sometimes tried to get Uma to visit her home. But her elder brother Gobindolal and her husband Peareymohan checked any such effort. Gobindolal felt that Uma was at the age where she should learn to respect her husband and settle herself in his home. Visits to her own home might distract her. He even wrote a profound article on the subject, and the readers had greatly appreciated it.

On getting to hear of it, Uma had written in her exercise book: "Elder brother, please take me home. I will never again make you cross with me."

One day, Uma was writing some such simple thing in her exercise book. She had closed the door from inside and that roused the curiosity of her sister-in-law Tilaka-manjari. "What does my sister-in-law do from time to time, closing the door?" she wondered. She peeped through a hole in the door and was most surprised to see Uma writing. Saraswati, the goddess of Learning, had never before come secretly to the inner quarters of their household. Kanaka-manjari, who was younger to Tilaka-manjari, also came and took a look.

The youngest - Ananga-manjari – stood on her toes and,

with great difficulty, looked into the mysterious scene. In course of her writing, Uma suddenly heard peals of familiar laughter from outside. She understood what had happened, and quickly shut her exercise book up in her box. In embarrassment and apprehension, she lay down on the bed, hiding her face.

When Peareymohan heard of this, he was most worried. He feared that in future Uma would be reading novels and neglecting domestic chores. He also had the theory that reading and writing reduced a woman's feminine powers, destroyed married life, and even led to widowhood. When he came home in the evening, he scolded Uma a lot and sarcastically commented: "I see I have to order a suit! My wife will be going to office with a pen stuck behind her ear!"

Uma could not understand exactly what he meant. She had not read Pearyemohan's article and had not yet developed the taste for such profundity. But she felt most shy and almost shrank within herself.

For a long time after that, she did not write anything in her exercise book. But one day, in the season after the monsoons when the Durga Puja takes place, she heard a beggar-woman on the road sing a song. It was a song about Durga coming to visit her parental place. As Uma is another name of Durga, the beggar was singing:

"Purobasi baley, Umar ma..

People were crying to Uma's mother: Your daughter has arrived.

Uma's mother, the queen, was rushing out to greet her daughter.

Uma was stretching out her arms and crying:

Why didn't you go and fetch me home?"

The song brought Uma's own homesickness to the fore. Her eyes filled with tears. Secretly calling the beggar-woman in, and closing the door, she began to take the song down in her exercise-book. She could not sing but ever since she had learnt to write, it was her habit to take down a song as soon as she heard it and so make up for her inability to sing.

But as Uma was writing the song down, her sisters-in-law, Tilaka-manjari, Kanaka-manjari and Ananga-manjari, peeped in through the hole in the door. Suddenly they began to laugh and clap: "Sister-in-law, we have seen everything that you are doing!"

At once opening the door, Uma began to plead with them: "Don't tell anyone, please! I'll never do it again. I'll never write again. Please don't tell anyone!" Then she noticed that Tilaka-manjari was eying her exercise book. She rushed and picked it up and pressed it to her chest. The sisters-in-law tried hard to wrest it away from her, but could not. Then they called their elder brother in. Uma's husband Peareymohan came in and sat down on the bed in a serious manner. In a thundering voice, he said: "Give me the exercise book."

When Uma did not obey him, he repeated his command in a lower tone: "Give it."

Pressing the exercise book to her chest, the girl looked most entreatingly at her husband's face. Peareymohan got up to grab it away from her. Then Uma threw the exercise book away on the ground and, hiding her face in her hands, lay down on the floor.

Peareymohan began to read out aloud from the exercise book. His sisters were in splits as he read and Uma tried to clutch the mother earth in a deeper embrace.

Uma never got her exercise book back.

Peareymohan too had such an exercise book like this but there was no one to confiscate it!

❐

5

Clouds and Sunshine

Megh O Roudra

1

It had rained the previous day and the sun and the clouds were chasing each other across the waving fields of paddy. In the nearby village of Tilkuchi, in an old house by the side of the road, a young man was sitting inside a room with a grilled window. Along the path just outside the window, a little girl in a striped *sari* was walking to and fro. She was carrying some *kala jamun* berries in the *anchal* of her *sari,* and eating them one by one.

The youth inside the room was engrossed in a pile of books, and the girl obviously knew him very well. But she was strutting about so as to give the impression that she was completely taken up with her berries and did not care a jot for the youth.

But the youth was not only absorbed in his book, but also had weak eyesight. He did not even see the girl and remained unaffected by her silent peevishness.

Ultimately, to attract his attention, the girl threw in a few of the seeds of the berries she was eating. As they hit the wooden door, the youth gave a start and looked up. He squinted and looked out with care. Recognizing the girl, he went up to the window and smilingly called out to the girl: "Giribala!"

Giribala walked on as if she had not heard.

The youth realized that he had somehow offended her. He quickly came out of the room and said, "Why, aren't you going to give me any berries today?"

These berries came from a tree in the compound of Giribala's house and she brought them for the youth every day. But today she seemed to forget that entirely! She acted as though she had picked them only for herself. But then, why carry them all the way to someone else's house and eat them in full view of that someone else?

The youth came and caught hold of Giribala's hands. Giribala twisted her little body here and there in an attempt to free herself. Then she suddenly burst into tears and ran away, scattering the berries from her sari on to the ground.

In the afternoon, the sun was playing among fluffy white clouds. The youth was sitting inside his room and Giribala was hovering outside his window. Only, the youth was no longer busy with his books. In fact, he was busy eating *kala jamun*, and occasionally flinging them outside. But was this fair? Giribala had come there once more, sacrificing her pride. Wasn't it cruel of the young man to ignore that move to make friends again?

Getting red in the face, Giribala began to go away. The young man now came out and caught her hands once more.

Once again - just as in the morning – Giribala tried to free herself from his grasp. But this time she did not cry. Instead, hiding her face in the youth's back, she laughed profusely, and allowed herself to be led into the room, as if only by force.

It was like the play of sunlight and shadows upon the earth.

2

The youth was named Shashishekhar, and he was a highly qualified person holding two degrees, M.A. and B.L. But in spite of his degrees in literature and law, Shashishekhar was not either efficient or interested in administrative work or property matters. He spent his time reading some English classics that he had.

Ten-year-old Giribala belonged to the same village. Her father Harakumar worked as a *nayeb* (administrative officer) of the local *zamindar* (landlord).

Giribala wanted to be able to read like her brothers who went to school while she did not. Books fascinated her. She wanted to unravel the mysteries she felt they contained. But her brothers refused to teach her how to read.

Shashishekhar poring over his books also fascinated her. For hours she would stand outside his window and watch him turn the pages of fat tomes.

One day this caught Shashishekhar's attention. "Come, Giribala, see the pictures in my books", he called out to her.

Giribala ran away the first few times, but eventually went in. Slowly, she became Shashishekhar's pupil. In the two years between eight and ten, she learnt to read Bengali as well as English primers. She listened to Shashishekhar re-telling old classics to her. Sometimes he even discussed the merits of books with her, and she participated in her small way in his critical appreciation of literature.

The rest of the village was absorbed in gossip, court cases and petty affairs. Shashishekhar and Giribala, unequal as they were in age and education, lived in their world of books.

3

Giribala's father Harakumar developed a dislike for Shashishekhar, as his degree in law was not of much use to him. He pestered the peace-loving Shashishekhar so much that he decided to leave the village.

Just then the Joint Magistrate, a Britisher, with his whole team of constables, horses, cooks and bearers pitched his tent near the village. Harakumar catered to every demand he made. But when he asked for four *seer*s of ghee for his dog, Harakumar raised a mild objection. The magistrate in his fury made him run around the village with a menial servant holding his ear. This public insult plunged Harakumar into deep depression. But Shashishekar felt his blood boil. "Bring a defamation case against the magistrate", he came up to Harakumar and urged. "I will fight the case as your lawyer."

4

Although he was shy and withdrawn by nature, Shashishekhar now arrived at the court to fight his case. The Magistrate tried to get him agree to a compromise. But Shashishekhar refused. However, the Joint Magistrate applied pressure on the landlord, who in turn applied pressure upon Harakumar, who buckled under at once. He said that he did not mind the `punishment' that had been given to him. It was Shashishekhar who had got him to bring a case against the Joint Magistrate.

"Has Shashi joined the Congress?" asked the Magistrate.

"Yes", lied Harakumar.

5

Meanwhile Shashishekhar had been seriously preparing

for his case. Giribala found him delving into a thick, black volume without any pictures in it. He never made any attempt to explain its contents to Giribala who came to regard it as a foe. Hurt, she stopped going to her `Shahs-dada' for a couple of days. When she went next, she found that her strategy had not worked at all. Shashishekhar had not noticed her absence and, standing in front of the grille of the window, was busy practicing some speech in English.

She tried to attract his attention by calling out to an imaginary friend: "Swarna, I am coming!" But even when she walked away, nobody came after her. Giribala felt so bad that she tore off her notes and scattered the torn pages on the ground. It grew cloudy. Giribala hid behind a tree and wept.

6

As Harakumar had settled his issue with the Joint Magistrate, Shashishekhar's performance as a lawyer was never needed. He had studied his laws and practiced his cross questions. All that was futile! He put his law book away, and suddenly realized that Giribala was absent. He remembered how she had been coming these days, only to be ignored. One day she had come with Bakul flowers wet with rain. But he had not bothered to look up from his book. She had then stopped coming in, but merely passed by the window. But even that was some days ago. What had happened now? Was she angry? Was she ill?

He found it difficult to concentrate on his old books of literature. He kept looking up to see if Giribala had come. Then he learnt that Giribala was no more allowed out of the house. Her wedding had been fixed.

In fact, even after tearing up her books of primers, Giribala had started out for Shashishekhar's house with small gifts of pickled lime and mango. But her father had forbidden her from going to her `Shashi-*dada*' again.

7

Harakumar had felt that in withdrawing the case, he had lost respect in Shashishekhar's eyes. He created problems for Shashishekhar, forcing him to leave the village. He did not even invite him for Giribala's wedding. In fact, as the *shahnai* was playing on the occasion of the wedding, Shashishekhar had taken a boat to Kolkata.

On his way, Shashishekhar saw that a boat piled with merchandise was trying to overtake a steamer. Full sail, it had even succeeded in moving ahead, when the manager of the steamer - a Britisher - shot out at the sails with his gun. The sail burst, the boat capsized, and the steamer vanished round the bend of the river. Shashibhushan was witness to the whole thing.

He went ahead on the boat he was on, and rescued all but one of the boatmen and passengers on the boat that had sunk. But his blood was boiling at the injustice of it all, and he urged the boatmen and passengers to bring a case against the manager of the steamer. They were scared and unwilling. (Those were the days of the British Raj.) They said they had seen nothing! Even then, Shashishekhar complained to the court. Nothing came out of it. The manager got away scot-free by saying that he had taken his shot at flying cranes and was completely unaware and innocent of shooting at what he called a `dirty rag', that is, the sail of the boat.

Shashishekhar left once more for Kolkata. On his way, he saw the boat of a District Superintendent of the Police move straight through the fishing net of some poor fishermen. It caused some minor inconvenience to the

Police Superintendent and, livid with anger, he ordered the fishing net to be cut into pieces and the fishermen to be arrested. The fishermen- innocent as they were - had run away. The policemen caught hold of some poor bystanders, and proceeded to take them away.

Shashishekhar could not bear such injustice. In his slippers and unbuttoned *kurta,* squinting through his glasses, he strode up to the Police Superintendent and shouted: "You have no right to do this!" The Police Superintendent shouted back an insult. Shashishekhar fell upon him and began to pummel him madly. He was caught, beaten unconscious, and locked up.

Shashishekhar was released on bail, but a case of assault was brought against him. Shashishekhar called upon the fishermen as his witnesses, but they were scared to testify against the powerful British police officer. Some people from his own village had been present on the occasion. They too refused to bear Shashishekhar out. He lost and was sentenced to five years of imprisonment.

\

Soon after Shashishekhar had gone to prison, he lost his father. He hardly had any relative to care for the property he had in the village. Harakumar cleverly took all that over.

8

Five long years went by. During those years, Shashishekhar suffered more than the usual hardened criminals and when he came out of the prison, he was broken both in health and spirits.

He had no home, no relatives, and no social circle to go back to. As he stood outside the prison walls, he felt completely at a loose end.

Just then a huge coach rolled up to him. A servant got down and asked if he was Shashishekhar Babu. "My employer has sent for you", he announced. Puzzled though he was, Shashishekhar got into the coach.

In the sky, the clouds and the sun were again at play, casting sun and shade over the fields that fell on either side of the coach as it proceeded through the countryside.

"*My friend of old times, come back*!" sang a beggar. Shashishekhar found himself humming to its tune, and even adding lines of his own.

"*Come back, my playful one,*

My tearful one, my joyful one,

Come back!"

The coach took him to a walled mansion. Unquestioningly, Shashishekhar followed the servant into a room in which stood tall glass cases full of neatly arrayed volumes of books. They had colorful covers with their titles embossed in gold. At the sight of those book-cases, Shashishekhar felt as though he had been released a second time from prison. There was also a table in the room. On it lay a cracked slate, and a few old exercise books with the name `Giribala Devi' written on them in thick letters in Shashishekhar's own handwriting!

Covering his face in his hands, Shashishekhar lay his head down on those books for a long time, remembering the old times beside a grilled window and with a little girl strolling outside.

A mild shuffle made him look up.

Giribala stood before him, with a silver platter of fruits and berries in her hand. As he looked up, she bent down on the ground and bowed to him.

She had no ornaments on and wore white.

She was a widow.

As she raised her eyes to the tired, broken-bodied Shashishekhar, tears began to course down her cheeks. Tears rose also to Shashishekhar's throat and choked all speech.

Outside, the beggar sang: *"Come back, old friend!"*

❐

6

The Postmaster

The first posting that the Postmaster got was in the newly established Post Office at the tiny village of Ulapur. There was an indigo plantation nearby and its Englishman planter had got this Post Office set up after a lot of effort.

The Postmaster hailed from the city of Kolkata and felt like a fish out of water in this village. His office was in a huge and dark mud hut near a pond that had jungle all around it and was itself green with vegetation. The employees at the plantation were very busy and anyway, not fit company for the city-bred young man. Nor did he know the art of mixing with village people. On the other hand, he did not have too much work to handle. He tried his hand at writing poetry. Although he sang the praise of nature in his poems, he would have been much relieved to find buildings rather than trees all around him.

His salary was very meager. He had to cook for himself and had an orphan girl doing other tasks for him in exchange for a few frugal meals. Ratan, as she was called, was about ten or twelve years in age, but hardly had any prospects of marriage.

In the evenings, when the smoke of mosquito repellents coiled up from the cow-sheds of the village, crickets sang in the bushes, and mendicant groups sang drunken music in their shelters, the Postmaster felt somewhat scared to sit alone in the darkness of his hut, watching the trembling trees. Lighting a small lamp in a corner of his room, he used to call out: "Ratan!"

"What is it, Babu (gentleman/master)", Ratan did not come immediately. "Why do you call me?"

"What are you at?"

"I am just going to light the kitchen fire - there is work in the kitchen -"

"Let the kitchen work be - you get me my tobacco."

Ratan used to come in soon, her cheeks puffed out, blowing at the fire at the end of the Postmaster's country-made pipe.

Snatching it from her, Postmaster started off a conversation with her." Well, Ratan, do you remember your mother?"

Yes and no, Ratan used to say. She remembered her father more. He had been more affectionate towards her. She also remembered a little brother whom she had played with. One memory came back to her more than the others - the memory of playing the game of fishing, sitting by a pond with her brother and pretending that a stick was their fishing rod.

Chatting like this, sometimes it grew late and then the Postmaster did not feel like cooking any more. Ratan quickly lit the fire, made a few *chapattis*. Leftover *sabzi* and *chapatti* served as dinner for both of them. On some other days, sitting on a wooden bed in that huge mud hut, the Postmaster began to talk of his own home. He talked of his mother, elder sister and younger brother - whom he missed so much in his village posting - but could not mention to the plantation employees. He found no problem in discussing them freely with this small, illiterate village girl. It came about that Ratan began referring to them as Ma (mother), Didi (elder sister) and Bhai (younger brother) – as if she had known them all her life. She even drew up sketches of them in the small canvass of her heart. From Babu, the postmaster too became Dada (elder brother)-babu.

One rainy afternoon the Postmaster had nothing to do and felt particularly like having some one of his own near him.

Sighing, he called out: "Ratan!"

Ratan was sitting under a nearby guava tree, legs outstretched, guava in hand.

She rushed up to her master. "Did you call me, Dada-babu?"

"I am going to teach you to read and write", said the Postmaster.

The whole afternoon passed by in introducing Ratan to the letters of the Bengali alphabet. Within a few days, Ratan mastered them and began to read and write complete words.

It was the month of Shravana. Monsoon was in full force. One rainy day, Ratan waited for long at the door for a call from her teacher the Postmaster, but the call never came. She finally went in with her books and stuff, only to find the Postmaster huddled in his wooden bed. "Ratan, I am not feeling too well", he called in a suffering tone. "Will you put your hand on my forehead and check if I have got fever?"

Ratan responded to this forlorn cry for family affection. She no longer remained just a small girl. From that instant she took up the position of a mother. She called the village doctor, administered the medicines to the Postmaster at the right hours, sat by the bedside all night, and of her own accord, cooked him his recommended diet. Every now and then she would ask:" Are you feeling a little better, Dada-babu?"

After a long spell of illness, the Postmaster recovered. He decided inwardly that enough was enough, and he had to get himself a different posting. Mentioning the local conditions, he immediately applied to the postal authority at Kolkata for a transfer.

Being relieved from her duties as a nurse, Ratan once again came out and occupied her old position by the door. But there were no calls for her as before. She peeped in some times, and found the Postmaster sitting or lying down most absentmindedly. Ratan waited for her call and the Postmaster waited for his transfer order. Sitting by the door, Ratan went over her old lessons a hundred times. She had the fear that she might mix up her spellings the day there was a sudden call for her.

After a week or so, indeed there was a call.

Ratan went in and asked, "Dada-babu, were you calling me?"

"Ratan, I am going away tomorrow itself", said the Postmaster.

"Where are you going, Dada-babu?" asked Ratan.

"I am going home".

"When will you be coming back?"

"I won't be coming back".

Ratan did not ask anything further. The Postmaster himself told her that he had applied for a transfer. The application had been rejected. So he was resigning his post and going home.

For a long time nobody said a word. In the flickering

lamplight, rain dropped down through a hole in the roof and collected in a bowl kept right under the hole.

After a while Ratan got up and went to the kitchen to make the *chapattis*. The task took longer than usual. After the Postmaster had eaten, the girl asked her: "Dada-babu, will you take me to your home?"

"How can that be!" said the Postmaster with a laugh. He did not even feel it necessary to explain to the girl why it was impossible.

All night through her sleep and wakeful hours, the girl heard his laughing words: 'How can that be!'

The Postmaster, like most people from Kolkata, had the habit of bathing not in the pond or river directly but in water that had been collected in a bucket.

Next morning as soon as he got up, he found the water ready and waiting for him. For some reason Ratan had not been able to ask him exactly when he would be going. So she had gone right in the night and fetched the water, and kept it ready for him.

Once the Postmaster had taken his bath, he called for Ratan. Ratan entered silently and looked at her master, awaiting his instruction.

"Ratan", said her master, "I'll talk to the man who will come in my stead. He will care for you just as I used to. You don't have to worry at all."

These words might have been kind but Ratan burst out crying: "No, no, you don't have to talk to anyone. I don't want to stay on." The Postmaster had never seen Ratan behave like this and was surprised.

The new Postmaster arrived. The old Postmaster handed over the charge to him and began to take his leave. He called Ratan and offered her some money. "Ratan, I have never been able to give you anything. Now, while leaving, I am giving you something. It will take care of you for a few days."

Keeping only the travel expenses with him, he took his whole salary out of his pocket. Ratan fell to the ground and caught hold of his feet.

"Dada-babu, please, you don't have to give me anything. Please, nobody has to think of me—"

With this, she ran away from there.

The ex-Postmaster sighed, and started off, with his tin box and umbrella.

As he mounted the boat, and as the boat started along the river swollen in monsoon, he felt a deep twinge of pain. "Let me go back and get that orphaned child along with me", he thought for a moment. But the boat was already on the move, and the Postmaster comforted himself with the theory: "Life is full of partings. What is the point of going back?"

But Ratan had no theories to comfort her. She just hung around the Post Office, tears flooding her face. A faint hope kept her tied to it: perhaps Dada-babu will come back?

❐

7

The Trouble

Aapad

It was a stormy night at Chandannagar, some way off the big city of Kolkata.

In a big garden resort by the river Ganga, Sharat Babu and his pretty wife Kiranmoyee were having a chat by the lamplight. They had come there on a recuperation trip. Kiranmoyee had been very ill and the village doctor had advised a change of air. Her devoted husband had not only sent her here but accompanied her himself. His mother too was fond of Kiranmoyee and come along with them.

Kiranmoyee had almost recovered but she was very bored in that small place. She was a social creature, naturally fond of company. She liked to have good fun and cheerful chit-chat. She was tired of medicines, hot compresses, diet and so on.

On this night, when the storm was raging over the swollen river, a sulky Kiranmoyee was asking her husband to end this rest cure and take her back to their native place.

Just then, there was a commotion outside the door. Kiran opened the door. A servant reported that somewhere on the river a boat had capsized and a Brahmin boy from that boat had saved himself by swimming across to their garden resort.

Kiran lost all her sulkiness and welcomed the boy in with dry clothes and a bowl of hot milk.

His name was Neelakanta. He had long hair, large eyes, and no trace of moustache as yet. Kiran sat right before him as he ate, and learnt that he was from a *jatra* or moving theatrical group. It was going to a nearby village to perform when a storm arose and the boat sank. Neelakanta was a good swimmer and so saved himself. But he had no idea what had happened to the rest of the group.

Kiran's heart went out to this youth who had had such a narrow escape from death. Her husband was happy at the thought that Kiran had found someone to absorb her attention and keep her occupied. As for Neelakanta, he was only too happy with the comfort and attention he received here, after the hardships of the life in the theatre group.

So it came about that Neelakanta stayed on at the garden resort. But soon Sharat Babu and his mother changed their opinion of him and began to regard him as an *aapad,* that is, a sudden trouble or problem.

Neelakanta began to take puffs at the long pipe that Sharat had for smoking tobacco. He began to calmly use Sharat's fancy silk umbrella as he went about looking for new friends in the locality. He picked up a stray dog as his pet and encouraged it so much that would come right in and put its dirty paws on the carpet in the living room. He gathered quite a following of local children and finished off all the unripe mangoes on the trees.

There was no doubt that Kiran spoilt the boy. She dressed him up in Sharat Babu's old dresses and socks, and gifted him with new *dhoti, chadar* and shoes, making a `babu' of him. Sharat Babu and his mother asked her not to, but she never listened. She often called Neelakanta up to her and made him act out scenes of plays before her. She sat on the bed chewing *paan* or betel leaves, with the maid drying her hair, and whiled away the long afternoons watching Neelakanta sing and wave his arms about in the role of female characters like Sita, Radha or Damayanti.

Sharat often boxed Neelakanta's ears or gave him a slap. But the boy did not seem to care. In his days at the theatre company, he had been used to far severe punishment.

He was about seventeen but looked like fourteen. Because he had acted in female roles at the theatre company, his development as a youth had been stunted. But now his teenage seemed to proceed more normally. He began to feel bad when Kiran asked him to act out female roles. He tried to pick up some lessons from the accountant in Sharat Babu's employment. But the accountant disliked Neelakanta for being such a pet of Kiran's, and anyway, Neelakanta did not have any power of concentration. Rather, he was a dreamer. The books he tried to read, or the plays he had acted in, filled his imagination with dreams - dreams in which figured the gracious lady who had given him refuge.

But within this imaginative and romantic personality there also persisted the long-haired Neelakanta who played female roles or stole mangoes and was slapped by Sharat.

Meanwhile, Satish, the younger brother of Sharat, landed up there for his holidays. Kiran was delighted. Between the brother-in-law and the sister-in-law there were pranks played, jokes exchanged and fun times enjoyed. Neelakanta suddenly felt bitter and out of sorts. He began to bully the local youngsters who followed him about. He often kicked the stray dog he had made his pet. As he walked along, he unnecessarily hit the mango trees with a stick. He did not eat to his fill if Kiran failed to be present while he ate -

something that began to happen quite often now. He cried himself to sleep, without knowing exactly why.

He felt Satish was all the time saying things against him to Kiran. He prayed that in the next birth he would be born as Satish and Satish as him. He cursed Satish as his ears rang with the merry peals of laughter that were ringing out as Satish sat upstairs with Kiranmoyee.

He did not dare to openly have a fight with Satish, but pestered him in petty ways. One day Satish had gone for his bath keeping a cake of soap on the embankment. When he reached out for the soap, he found it gone. Another day, he found a favourite shirt of his float away along the river. Yet another day, Kiran called up Neelakanta and to amuse Satish, asked him to sing a song from the plays he used to perform. To her surprise, Neelakanta refused.

At last it was time for Kiranmoyee to go. She was now fully recovered. Satish too, would, as a matter of course, be going with them. But no one even bothered to think of what Neelakanta would do - whether he would go with them or stay on here. Nobody was bothered.

Kiran proposed that Neelakanta should go with them to their own place. Her husband, mother-in-law and brother-in-law, all three protested. Kiran had to call Neelakanta up and in a few sweet words, ask him to return to his own village.

After the neglect of days, these sweet words made Neelakanta burst out crying. Tears came into Kiran's eyes also. She felt guilty at showering someone with temporary affection when he could not be given anything permanent.

Satish ridiculed Neelakanta for his show of emotions, and reproached Kiran," "You are too trustful of everyone! An unknown character lording it over here; he is just shamming so that your heart melts and he does not have to lose all this comfort."

Neelakanta hurried away, bleeding inwardly.

Satish had a very fancy inkstand shaped like a swan. Kiran often teased him about it. One day before departure, it could not be found anywhere. Kiran tried to make a joke of it by saying: "Your swan has flown off somewhere". But an angry Satish accused Neelakanta of stealing it. Hauling him up before everyone, including Kiranmoyee, he shouted:

"Get me back my inkstand!"

Kironmoyee took Neelakanta aside and said in a low, soft voice: "Neelu, if you have indeed taken the inkstand, quietly give it back to me, and no one will ever know."

Neelakanta hid his face in his hands and wept.

Kiran came back and told the others: "Neelakanta cannot have stolen the inkstand."

"None other than Neelakanta has stolen it", said Sharat and Satish. They wanted to conduct a search of his room and his tin box. Kiran refused to let them. With tears in her eyes, she said, "If you question him or search his room, I will never again speak to you. You cannot doubt the innocent."

In the evening Kiranmoyee quietly entered the room Neelakanta had been allotted. She had got some new clothes and a ten-rupee note to give him. She wanted to quietly leave her affectionate gift inside the tin box which she herself had once given to the boy. With a key she had, she opened the box. But it was full of odds and ends like kites, pen-knife, broken bits of glass, apart from clothes. Kiranmoyee had to take everything out in order to make room for her gifts.

As she did so, she saw the inkstand lying at the bottom of the box, below everything. Stunned, red-faced, Kiran sat there holding the inkstand.

She did not get to know that Neelakanta too had entered from behind and caught sight of her sitting with the inkstand in her hand. Neelakanta thought that Kiran had come to search his box secretly and found him out as guilty. But how could he make her understand that he had not really wanted to steal the inkstand, but wanted only to teach Satish a lesson. He was not a thief! But then, what *was* he? Kiran had suspected him to be a thief. How could he bear such cruel injustice!

Kiran herself gave a long sigh, and put everything back in the tin box, with her gifts on top.

But the next day no trace could be found of Neelakanta. Neither the villagers nor the police could search him out. "Now let us search his box", suggested Sharat.

"Never!" said Kiran. Later she took the box into her room, took out the inkstand and dropped it into the Ganga in secret.

Sharat went away from Chandannagar with his whole family. Within a day, the garden resort became deserted. Only the stray dog that had become Neelakanta's pet lingered by the riverside, howling as he searched on.

❒

8

The Guest

Atithi

Motilal Babu was traveling along the river with his family to Kanthalia, a place in rural Bengal of which he was the *zamindar* or landlord.

As his boat halted at mid-day, and everyone got down to cook and lunch by the riverside, a *brahmin* youth of about fifteen or sixteen came up to him.

He wanted a lift up to Nandigram which the boat would be passing. Motilal Babu agreed and offered him lunch as well.

The youth, named Tarapada, had large eyes and a most pleasant look although his *dhoti* was old and faded. He had easy ways and immediately joined in the cooking. Then he took a dip in the river and got into a fresh *dhoti*.

Motilal Babu now took him inside the boat. His wife Annapurna and his nine-year-old daughter Charushashi were there and Annapurna's heart went out to Tarapada. 'How can his mother stay apart from this beautiful child of hers!' she thought to herself.

She placed two mats side by side for Motilal Babu and Tarapada. She pressed Tarapada to eat a lot but found that he resisted all the pressure – most pleasantly. He was neither shy nor obstinate but ate only as much as he wanted to. After lunch, Annapurna tried to extract some information about his background. All that she could gather was that at the age of seven or eight he had left home of his own accord.

"Isn't your mother living?"

"She is".

"Doesn't she love you?"

Tarapada considered this question so strange that he laughed. "Why shouldn't she love me?"

"Then why did you leave her?" asked Annapurna.

"She has four other sons and three daughters", said Tarapada.

"What a thing to say!" Annapurna was hurt. "Because one has five fingers, can one let one go?"

Tarapada was the fourth child of his parents and had lost his father very early in life. Even though he had several brothers and sisters, Tarapada was a very well-loved child. Not just his mother and siblings but neighbours too were most affectionate to him. Even his teacher at school spared him the rod.

Under such circumstances, there was no need for Tarapada to run away from his village. But he did do so, with a traveling theatre group that had come to perform at his village.

The villagers searched him out and brought him back. His mother and sisters wept to get him back, his elder brother reproached him affectionately. Neighbors too were very glad to have him back.

But Tarapada had an inborn urge to break out of bonds, bonds even of affection. So he ran away again and again till his family and neighbours gave up on him.

First he had joined a theatre group. The owner soon became

very fond of him and even the households that invited the theatre group to perform before them took note of this lovely child and specially invited him over. But one fine morning Tarapada just vanished.

He joined a group of traveling minstrels. The leader of the group taught him several songs and came to regard him as his own. But Tarapada disappeared again. At a village fair, Tarapada began to assist a vendor, and then a gymnastic group from Kolkata. Tarapada had taught himself to play the flute. At the gymnastic displays, his job was to play the *banshee* or bamboo flute at a fast rhythm, as an accompaniment to the performance of the gymnasts.

It is from this gymnastic group that he had escaped last. He was on his way to Nandigram, where the landlord was setting up a new theatre company and then he ran into Motilal Babu. Although Tarapada had seen a lot of the world, he had an innocence of his own that was untouched. Charmed by that innocence in his looks, mature and worldly-wise as Motilal Babu was, he welcomed him in with open arms.

As the boat journeyed along the river, Tarapada went up to the sail and watched the landscape on either side. He soon became friendly with the boatmen and even joined in the rowing. When the boatman needed to smoke, he took over his job and even did it ably!

In the evening Annapurna asked him what he liked to have for dinner." Whatever I get", Tarapada said with a kind of indifference. "Sometimes I don't even have dinner."

Annapurna got milk and sweets from the village they were passing. Tarapada took a very limited dinner and actually refused the milk. Even to Motilal Babu's pleading, he said:" I don't like milk."

A couple of days went by on the boat. Tarapada joined in the activities of getting provisions, cooking and rowing the boat. He did so spontaneously and efficiently. Whatever he saw, he looked at with interest. Whatever task came up before him, he took up with keenness. His eyes and his fingers were ever alert and active. But at the same time he was indifferent and unattached to the world around him.

He had a good memory because his brain was uncluttered by thoughts. He remembered the scenes he had seen enacted by the theatre groups he had joined and could act them out, songs and all.

One evening, Motilal Babu was reading out the *Ramayana* to his wife and daughter. Tarapada was so enthused at this that he came down from the roof of the boat, and said: "Keep the book down. Listen to me as I act out the story of Kush and Lav."

With a flute-like voice he sang and enacted the scenes. The boatmen were attracted and gathered in the room. People from passing boats tried to listen as long as they could. Annapurna felt like hugging the child and Motilal Babu felt that if he could make Tarapada stay, it would fulfill his need for a son.

Only, small Charushashi's heart felt like bursting with envy and resentment.

Charushashi was the only child of her parents and the only claimant to their affection. She was most whimsical and often threw tantrums over any dress or hairstyle that she did not fancy. At other times she was most demonstrative of her affections, kissing and hugging her mother to distraction.

She was a riddle.

Towards Tarapada, she developed a sharp and forceful

antipathy. She made her parents quite worried as well. She would push away her food, almost crying. She criticized the cooking and hit the maid. She complained unnecessarily about everything. The more Tarapada's qualities attracted and pleased - her as well as others - the angrier she grew.

The day Tarapada sang from the *Ramayana*, Annapurna asked her daughter, "So, Charu, how did you like it?" Charu shook her head hard. No, she had not liked it one bit, and was never going to like it either!

Realizing that Charu was growing jealous of Tarapada, her mother stopped praising him before her. Only when Charu fell asleep, did she, with her husband, sit at the door, while Tarapada performed on the deck of the boat. Even then Charu would sometimes get up from the bed and come out crying. "Ma, what a racket you are all making! I can't go to sleep." She found it intolerable that her parents were entertaining themselves with Tarapada's songs after sending her off to sleep.

This bright-eyed girl intrigued and amused Tarapada. He tried to win her over by telling her stories, playing the flute to her or singing her songs. But somehow he never was successful. The only thing that Charu seemed to like about him was his skill at swimming. At noon, when his fair body played among the blue waters, Charu would surreptitiously look up from the knitting she was doing sitting on the boat.

Tarapada did not even notice when the boat passed Nandigram by. After ten more days of journey, the boat reached Kanthalia. At the return of the landlord, the village held a big welcome ceremony. While it was on, Tarapada quickly got down from the boat, made a quick survey of the village and familiarized himself with the place and its people. Within a few days he stole the village's heart away.

This he did with the naturalness of his behaviour with all. He was a kid with kids, and mature yet respectful with the elderly. As he sat, say, in a sweet shop, he would wave away the flies from the sweets. As he sat with the potter, he would take a turn at the wheel. He knew a little of everything and brought the whole village under this control.

But Charushashi did not come under his control and perhaps that is why Tarapada stayed on in this particular place far beyond his usual number of days at any one place.

Charushashi had a friend named Sonamoni, a child-widow. She had been ill and unable to visit Charu for some days. When she finally came, Charu began to tell her of their newly-acquired jewel. Perhaps she had intended to impress her friend and arouse her curiosity. But she learnt that Sona was already quite familiar with Tarapada, who had often visited her, plucked fruits and flowers for her and even made a small bamboo flute. She called him `Dada' or elder brother. Tarapada called her mother Mashi (Aunty) in the easy way he had. Charu felt the tingle of jealousy all over her body. She had regarded Tarapada as their very own, very private possession, with which she could sometimes favour others. Why should he be already available to Sonamoni as her `Dada'?

On a most minor issue, Charu quarreled badly with Sonamoni. Then she went into Tarapada's room, threw his flute upon the floor, and jumped up and down on it. Just then, Tarapada came upon the scene. "Why are you smashing up my flute?" he asked in surprise.

"I'm doing the right thing", cried Charu, red-faced and red-eyed. Then she jumped upon it some more times, burst into tears and ran away. Tarapada picked up the flute and burst out laughing at the condition it was in. With every day that passed, Charu became more of a mystery to him.

Tarapada could not read English but felt drawn to the beautifully illustrated volumes of books in Motilal Babu's library. He used to turn their pages and look at their pictures with such interest that Motilal Babu asked: "Do you want to learn English?"

"Yes" said Tarapada eagerly.

He threw himself into the study of English with fervor, giving up interaction with people. He did not go out much. Sometimes the village kids saw him walking up and down the deserted riverside, trying to memorise poetry. They were too scared of him to interrupt him. Earlier he used to eat with the family and Annapurna took delight in feeding him. Now he requested for food to be brought outside so that there was less of a break in his studies. Annapurna objected but Motilal Babu saw a point in it.

Charu suddenly threw a tantrum. She too would learn English from a tutor! But she had no concentration and only created a disturbance in Tarapada's study. She never learnt her own lessons but cried and sulked if Tarapada mastered his own and went on to the next. She had to be taught the same even though she was way behind. In his leisure hours Tarapada sat and practiced his lessons in his own room. Charu secretly entered the room and spilt ink upon his exercise books, tore off pages from his book or stole off his pen. Tarapada treated all this with amused tolerance and hit her when he could not bear any more. But he could not bring Charu under control.

One day he found pages of his exercise covered with ink, and sat silent and sad. Charu came at the door and hovered there, expecting to be beaten. But Tarapada just sat, silent and sad. This was a very effective punishment. Soon Charu wrote out an apology and tried to draw Tarapada's attention to it. At the sight of those big unformed letters saying she was sorry, Tarapada burst out laughing. Charu ran away in anger and embarrassment.

A couple of times Sonamoni had come and peeped into the study, which was in the outer part of the house. Charu was still a friend, but not in respect of Tarapada. So Sonamoni chose to come only when Charu was inside the house. Tarapada would ask affectionately, "What news, Sona?"

"My mother has asked you to drop in one day", Sona would say timidly.

"Tell Mashi, I will", Tarapada would say. Suddenly Charu would turn up and scare Sonamoni away:" How dare you come and disturb him? I'll complain to my father that you are creating a racket while he is studying!"

Tarapada did pay Sonamoni's mother a couple of visits. But after that Charu locked his door from outside, opening it only at dinner time. An enraged Tarapada threatened to leave without having his dinner. With folded palms Charu then pleaded him to stay. When that did not work, she burst into such wild weeping that Tarapada had to give in.

Two years went by in this fashion. Tarapada had never allowed himself to be tied down anywhere as long as this. Perhaps he had got really interested in his studies, or was developing the usual tendency to settle down and be comfortable in life, or perhaps he had started to have feelings in his heart for his unruly classmate. But he was staying on.

Meanwhile Charushashi reached the age of eleven years, in those days and circumstances, a marriageable age. Motilal Babu began to look for suitable bridegrooms, and as was the prevalent custom, restricted Charu from going out and studying English.

Charu rebelled, and her mother said to Motilal Babu, "Why are you looking here and there for a bridegroom. Tarapada is quite suitable and your daughter too likes him."

"But I know nothing of Tarapada's background", protested a surprised Motilal Babu. "How can I marry my only child off like that? I want a good match for her."

He did find a good match but the day the bridegroom's party came to see Charu, she refused to appear before them. To prevent a scene, Motilal Babu had to cook up some excuse. He now began to think that Tarapada would not be such a bad choice for Charu. That way, he and his wife would be spared the pangs of separation from their daughter, and she, any criticism from in-laws.

Enquiries were made about Tarapada's family. The report was that it was a good family but very poor. A formal proposal was then sent to Tarapada's mother and older brothers who did not think twice about accepting it and accepted it most happily.

At Kanthalia, wedding arrangements began to be made, although Motilal Babu, a circumspect man, did not let it spread.

But Charu could not be contained. Like a gang of robbers, she would sometimes descend upon Tarapada's study and disturb its peace - sometimes affectionate, sometimes angry. But now Tarapada began to feel an electrifying thrill in such doings. Ever light-hearted, ever-unattached, now he began to get unmindful and have daydreams. Sometimes he left his textbooks and went into the library and turned the pages of books with colourful illustrations, dreaming dreams of his own that were even more colourful. It never occurred to him to laugh at Charu or beat her up when she pestered him. This subtle change of attitude, this feeling of being bound and attached, seemed a new dream of himself.

Deciding upon a particular date, Motilal Babu sent people to fetch Tarapada's mother and brothers by boat. But he did not let Tarapada know about it. He asked his lawyer in Kolkata to arrange a musical band to play on the occasions and also sent him a list of required provisions for the ceremony.

Monsoon arrived. The river was swollen with rain-water. This was the time for a big annual fair at Kurulkata, the next *zamindari* area. Going to the river on a moonlit night, Tarapada saw numerous boats floating along it towards Kurulkata. One boat carried the giant wheel, another carried goods for sale, and yet another, a traveling theatre group. From some boats came the music of some concert party from Kolkata, from some there came the clash of cymbals from some singing group beyond Bengal. The air was charged with excitement. Soon it became even darker with rain clouds covering up the moon. The village of Kanthalia slept on in that darkness.

Next morning Tarapada's mother and elder brothers arrived. Three other boats too arrived, carrying wedding gifts and equipment. Carrying some sweets and pickles, Sonamoni too came and peeped timidly into Tarapada's study.

But Tarapada could not be seen the next morning.

Before the bonds of love, affection and domestic life could completely encircle him, the guest of Kanthalia had left, with the heart of everybody at Kanthalia.

❒

A Boy and A Plant

Balai

Human being is the end-product of a long process of evolution. There are elements of birds and beasts and even plants and other living organisms in a human being.

In my brother's motherless child Balai, plants were the dominant element.

From his very childhood, he had the habit not of running around but being still and staring at the world around him – like the plants do. When it rained, his entire body seemed to hear its pitter-patter. When the afternoon sunrays fell on the rooftop, he bared his body to it and walked about. He was not a talkative child. He had large eyes and silently looked out of them at the surrounding nature.

Once I had taken him to the hills. In front of our house there was a grassy slope going down the hillside. It thrilled Balai. He rolled down it, as though he was part of the slope going down. As he went down, the grasses would tickle the back of his neck, and he would laugh merrily.

When it rained in the night and the morning light fell upon the tall trees of the mountains, Balai would go and stand quietly among them in wonder.

His eyes were lost in thought. It is not that they were always looking upwards – towards the sun or the clouds. They were often cast down as if looking for something. They were keen to see the new saplings raise their heads out of the earth, and seemed to have a conversation going on with them. Perhaps the young shoots asked Balai: "What is your name? " Or, "Where is your mother?" Perhaps Balai replied: "My mother is gone." It hurt him when people plucked flowers from trees. He had realized that this made no sense to others and so he tried to hide it. Kids of his age threw pebbles up at trees to bring fruits down. Balai could not say anything to them openly but he turned his face away and moved elsewhere. To tease him, his friends, while walking through a garden, would swing a stick at the flowerbeds on either side or unnecessarily break off a branch from a tree. Balai felt like crying but was embarrassed to do so in case it was seen as madness.

The days he suffered most were those of trimming the lawn. Everyday he spotted tiny flowers among the grasses, yellow and mauve and without any names. Everyday he found new sapling shooting up from seeds that had perhaps been blown there by the wind. How pretty they were! How delicate! But because they were not fancy plants, there was no one to hear their cries as they were cut down by the *ghasiara* (grass-cutter).

On some days, he came and sat on his aunt's lap and put his arms around her neck as he appealed: "Kaki, why don't you tell the *ghasiara* not to cut off my plants."

"What nonsense you speak, Balai", my wife would say. "They are wild growth and must be trimmed."

And so Balai had gathered that there were some feelings that were entirely his own, that he could not share with anyone else. Balai seemed get a message straight from nature that every blade of grass, every sapling, every bit of creation wanted to live, survive and grow. We had laughed a lot at this absurd idea.

One day I was reading the newspaper when Balai excitedly took me to the garden. Right in the middle of the gravel path across the garden, a sapling of Shimul (silk-cotton) had shot up.

Alas, Balai had made a mistake in calling me out and showing me the sapling. He had spotted it right from the day it had sprung up from the ground. He had watered it everyday, watched over it morning and afternoon. Silk-cotton trees grow fast – but not as fast as Balai's keen interest in its growth. When it had grown about two feet tall, and sprouted a wealth of leaves, Balai was struck with awe and admiration. Every mother is overwhelmed when her baby makes the first movements that indicate growth. She thinks it is a wonder child that she has got. Balai had thought the same, and brought me out to get me impressed as well.

"I must tell the gardener to uproot it and throw it away."

Balai gave a big start. What a terrible thing for his uncle to have said!

"Please, Kaka, no! Please don't uproot it!"

"What nonsense you speak, Balai! It is right in the middle of this gravel path. When it grows up it will send out puffs of cotton on all sides and create a mess."

When he could not cope with me, Balai appealed to his aunt. Getting on to her lap, he sobbed, "Kaki, you tell Kaka not to cut off the plant." He had thought of the right way out. His aunt said, "Do you hear? Come on, let his plant be."

I let it be.

Balai would have done better not to show that plant to me at all. Perhaps I would not even have noticed it. But now my eyes fell upon it every day. Within the year the plant grew up in a most unabashed fashion. And it was the tree Balai grew to be fondest of.

I felt the plant looked most stupid and audaciously out of place. Twice again I proposed its death sentence. I tempted Balai with cuttings of rose bushes. I offered him a new silk-cotton tree to be planted at another part of the garden, near the boundaries. But every time I suggested cutting it down, Balai gave a start of horror, and his aunt spoke out on his behalf: " It does not look so bad, come on!"

My sister-in-law, Balai's mother, had died when Balai was but a baby. My elder brother in his grief had gone abroad for higher education, leaving Balai with us. That is how Balai had grown up with us, his childless uncle and aunt. After a decade, my brother came back and took Balai away from us to give him a better education, first in Shimla and then in England. Tearfully, Balai left us to our emptiness. Two years passed by. Balai's aunt often wept for him secretly and handled Balai's old toys and pictures books, which she had preserved in the room that used to be his.

One day I happened to notice that the silk-cotton tree had grown so big that it could not be tolerated any more. I called the gardener and had it chopped off.

It so happened that soon after, Balai wrote a letter to his aunt asking for a photograph of the tree to be sent to him.He was going abroad and would not be able to see us before he went. So he wanted to take along with him a photograph of his friend – the tree.

"Call a professional photographer", said his aunt to me as she gave me Balai's letter written in his childish hand.

"Get Balai's tree photographed".

"But that tree has been chopped off!" said I.

For two days Balai's aunt did not partake of food and for many days after that she did not speak a word to me. She was wounded to the core – first by Balai's father taking him away and now by his uncle getting rid of his tree.

For, that tree had been to her a symbol of his life, a second Balai.

❐

10

Eloquent

Subha

When the newborn girl was named Subhashini, who knew that she would turn out to be speech-impaired, or simply, dumb? Her elder sisters had been named Sukeshini (One with Lots of Hair) and Su-hasini (One with a Nice Smile). To rhyme with those names, this one was named Su-bhashini (One Who Can Speak Well or, Eloquent).Now everyone called her Su-bha for short.

The two elder sisters had been duly married off. But Subha was unmarried as yet, a silent load weighing upon her parent's minds.

People do not generally remember that even when someone cannot speak, they can nevertheless hear and feel. So people openly expressed their worries about her, and discussed her right in front of her. From her very childhood Subha had come to understand that her birth was a curse upon her family. As a result she always tried to keep herself hidden from public view. It would be a relief if people forgot about me, she used to think. But she was always there in her parents' thought – as a painful problem.

Subha's mother was generally a little irritated with her, as though in some way she reflected some shortcoming of herself as a mother. But Subha's father Banikanttha had a soft corner for her.

Subha had no power of speech, but she had two large, dark eyes with long lashes and lips that trembled at the slightest twinge of emotion. Dark eyes have their own power of expression.

The village in which Subha lived was named Chandipur. It was on the bank of a small river and Banikantha's house was right by the riverside. It was a prosperous household, with cowshed and mango grove, bamboo fencing and haystack.

Whenever Subha found the time, she used to come and sit by the riverside. Nature used to make up for her lack of speech. Nature spoke for her – in terms of the gurgle of the waves, the songs of the birds, the murmur of trees, the footfall and talk of people all around. All of it seemed in some way to be the speech that Subha could not make.

At mid-day when the boatmen had their meals, householders took their nap, and even birds fell silent, Subha used to sit under the trees and watch the world through her large, long-lashed eyes. Nature and Subha would be alone in each other's mute company.

It is not as though Subha did not have a few friends of her own. There were two cows – Sarvashi and Panguli – who knew her very footsteps and responded lovingly to the way she folded her arms around them and rubbed her cheeks against their ears. Gazing at her affectionately, they licked her body. Every now and then Subha would go to the cowshed. The days she heard some bitter comment or reproach, she used to go there. Sensing something, they would come closer and rub their horns against her arms, as if to comfort her.

There was a goat and a kitten as well, which she petted. Then there was a creature of a higher order - Pratap – the youngest of the family of the Gosains. Pratap Gosain was a useless fellow. His parents had given up hope of his helping the family by taking up some steady job. His main activity was fishing. One can spend a lot of time sitting by the waters with one's fishing rod. That is what Pratap did, and that is how Subha and he often came to meet. Pratap felt good in people's company. But for someone who is fishing, a silent friend is the best. So Pratap came to value Subha's silent companionship. He began to call her `Su' rather than Subha – the name by which everybody else called her.

Subha used to sit under the Tamarind tree and Pratap used to sit with his fishing rod. A *paan* was Pratap's everyday quota and Subha made this betel-nut preparation herself and brought it along for him. She wished that Pratap would ask her for some special help. She wished for Pratap to see that she too could be of some use to the world.

But Pratap needed no help and never asked her to do anything for him. Then Subha used to pray to God for some magic powers that would give Pratap a big surprise and make him exclaim: "I never knew Subhi had such abilities!"

Suppose, for instance, that Subha was a mermaid, coming up from the river's depths, and leaving a jewel on the riverbank. Pratap then would dive in search for more, and come upon an underwater palace. Subha let her imagination go further. Pratap, she imagined, he would come upon the princess of that land under the river, and then find that it was none other than Subha!

But nothing so fantastic happened, and gradually Subha grew into a young woman as distinct from a girl. She felt the tide of youth flood her body. When it was full moon, she would often find herself open the door of her room and timidly step out. The moonlit night stretched silently before and Subha stood silently gazing at it.

Meanwhile Subha's parents had realized that it was high time for their daughter to get married. Village people were gossiping. In fact, they were thinking of making Banikanttha a social outcast because he had not married off his daughter even though she had grown-up.

Banikanttha and his wife discussed the matter at length. Banikanttha was away from the village for a while. Then he came back and asked his family to go to Kolkata with him. Preparations for the journey began. Subha's heart filled with a vague dread. Like a dumb animal she stayed by her parents' side. Looking into their faces with her large eyes, she tried to understand something. But they never explained anything to her.

One afternoon, however, Pratap looked up from his fishing and said with a smile: "Subha, I heard that a match has been found for you and you are going away to get married. Don't forget us, though!" Then he looked away again and concentrated on his fishing.

Subha looked at him like a stricken deer looking at the hunter. Silently she seemed to say: 'What wrong did I do to you?' She did not sit under the tree anymore. She went up and sat down at her father's feet. Banikanttha had had his nap and was having a smoke. Subha looked into his face and began to cry. Banikanttha tried to comfort her but tears came to his own eyes as well.

The day of departure was fixed. Subha went to the cowshed to take leave of her childhood friends. She fed Sarvashi and Panguli herself, put her arms around their necks and gazed into their eyes with eyes full of unspoken words. Tears fell from her long-lashed eyes.

That night Subha left her room and went out to the moon-washed river-bank. She fell upon the ground under the trees. Clutching at the earth, she tried to pray to Mother Nature not to let her go, but stretch out her hand like herself and clutch her to her breast.

On going to Kolkata, Banikanttha took up a temporary accommodation and presented Subha before a possible match for her.

His wife tied up Subha's hair in golden ribbons, covered her up with ornaments, and obliterated her natural beauty as much as she could. Tears coursed down Subha's cheeks. Her mother scolded her because that would make her eyes get swollen and ugly. But scolding could not make the tears stop.

The bridegroom himself, along with a friend, came to interview Subha. Subha kept on crying. But this enhanced her value to the bridegroom. It made him think: 'The girl has a soft heart and one day that may of use to me.' After looking at Subha for a long time, he pronounced: "Not bad". A suitable day was determined according to astrological calculations. Depositing their dumb daughter to an alien household, the parents went back to their village. They had met the requirements of social traditions.

The bridegroom was employed at a distance from Kolkata, in the central provinces. Immediately after the wedding, he took his bride there.

Within a week everyone got to understand that the newly-wedded bride was speech-impaired, dumb. Nobody understood that it was not her fault. She had not deceived anyone. Her eyes had said everything but nobody had been able to understand it. Subha looked here and there. Wherever she looked, she found no one who could understand the language of the dumb. She could not see the familiar faces she had known since her birth. In the silent heart of the young girl, there rang out an inarticulate cry that no one but God could hear.

This time her husband used both his ears and eyes and chose a bride endowed with the power of speech.

❒

11

Keeping the Vow

Pan-raksha

Banshi loved his younger brother Rashik with a love rare even in mothers. If Rashik was a little late in coming back from school, Banshi left his work and went looking for him. He could not eat without ensuring that Rashik ate first. Rashik's slightest illness had Banshi's tears flowing.

Rashik was sixteen years younger than Banshi and brought up entirely by him. The parents had died when Rashik was a toddler. So had the other siblings.

Banshi was a weaver. Weaving was their family trade. The family had once been prosperous. But the British had flooded India with mill-made textiles and ousted hand -woven textiles. Weavers were suffering from lack of demand.

But an affluent household in their locality Thanagarh kept Banshi provided with ample orders for his woven stuff.

Among the weavers of that locality, the custom was that the bridegroom had to pay a certain promised amount called `pan' to get himself a bride. Banshi could have put together the money to pay the *`pan'* for a bride of his own.

But all his money went in buying fancy clothes for Rashik. He provided small luxuries for his younger brother, cutting down on his own expenses.

Because Rashik was being brought up in such style, he was quite a hero to the other kids of the village who had no such luck. Also, Rashik had a certain knack in picking up new skills, although he soon lost interest in whatever he had picked up. When craftsmen from the city of Kolkata had come to put up a show of fireworks for the babu of Thanagarh, Rashik had quickly learnt their craft. For the next two years, he had taken care of the fireworks display in his locality at the time of Kali Puja. But by the third year, his interest had shifted to picking up `*thumri*' songs from Lucknow on a harmonium.

These traits of Rashik's impressed the villagers, and overwhelmed his own brother. "It is a wonder that such a child has come to be born in our family!" he used think, his eyes filling with tears at the thought. "All I want is for him to survive".

As Rashik crossed thirty, he got the idea getting him married. "It is better that Rashik carries on the family line", he thought. He began to look around the village for a girl Rashik could marry.

Well, Rashik had no dearth of girls to marry. All the village girls adored him. When he made clay dolls, the girls fought among themselves as to who should get them. Among them, there was a girl named Saurabhi who was very quiet and loved to watch Rashik as he fashioned his clay dolls. Often she helped him by reaching out clay and sticks to him. She brought *paan* for him, to supply whenever he asked. Once the dolls were finished, Rashik would ask: " Sairi, tell me which doll you would like." Shy Sairi would keep quiet. Banshi would then put a doll of his own choice into her hands. Once Rashik lost interest in clay modeling, it was playing the harmonium that took his fancy. All the other kids used to fall upon Rashik's harmonium, itching to play it. Rashik growled at them to keep them away. But to Saurabhi - who sat quietly watching - he would offer the chance himself. Banshi decided that he would arrange a match between Rashik and Saurabhi, But he knew that the *`pan'* or promised amount for her would be high - not less than Rs 500. For, Saurabhi's father was higher-up in the social scale.

So far Banshi had never asked Rashik to help him in his task of weaving. He had been happy to see Rashik occupied with his useless amusements.

Rashik for his part had found Banshi's occupation the dullest. Because Banshi was very frugal so far as his own food and clothes were concerned, Rashik thought him to be a miser. In fact, encouraged by Banshi himself, Rashik considered himself to be a creature superior to his own elder brother.

Meanwhile, Banshi was getting impatient to gather together the money for Rashik's wedding. He dreamt of the lights and decorations, and pressed on with his work. Yet his savings were growing only slowly, and Banshi was getting fatigued with the back-breaking work he was putting in.

He worked on even at night. He put off the buying of a new coverlet for himself although he needed it badly. He grew ill and weak. At last he called Rashik and asked him to help him in his work. "I cannot manage all the weaving by myself", he appealed. Rashik made a wry face.

Ill-health had put Banshi in a bad mood. He began to scold Rashik. "What is going to happen to you if you forsake your family occupation and go round having a roaring good time?"

Rashik took this reproach as a very severe one. He refused to eat at home and sulked all day by himself. Later in the day, feeling hungry, he asked Saurabhi to get him some snacks. Delighted, the little girl went home and brought him lots of puffed rice.

The next day Banshi in a way forced Rashik to sit down at the loom. This, he said, was their way of life, a family duty, not a matter of likes and dislikes.

But Rashik - so deft as picking up other skills - turned out to be a dud so far as weaving was concerned. The yarn got torn every now and then and the work hardly moved forward. At the thought of his admirers seeing him settling down in this mundane family trade, Rashik felt angry and embarrassed.

Banshi informed him through a friend that he was arranging his match with Saurabhi. Banshi had thought that this would please Rashik. But Rashik reacted in a perverse way. He stopped all his friendly interaction with the quiet little girl. Saurabhi lost her special claim on the harmonium as well as her privilege of fetching and carrying for Rashik. Her heart grew heavy. Rashik had once belonged completely to the village but now he felt himself yearning for the wider world. Banshi did not make him work for long hours. But even the few hours Rashik put in, spoilt the day for him.

Around this time, a youth from the rich Thanagarh household bought himself a bicycle. Rashik requested to be allowed to try it, and in a matter of hours mastered the art of cycling superbly. The bicycle became a pair of wings for him - like some divine weapon of the epics. It gave him a tremendous sense of freedom, of elation.

Rashik felt that without a bicycle, life was futile. And it was not so expensive, was it? Only a hundred and twenty-five rupees! In fact, thought Rashik, it was quite cheap!

He had decided never to ask his brother for anything again.

But the bicycle made him break that vow. Of course, he put his plea as though it was a request for a loan. "You have to lend me a hundred and twenty-five rupees", he told Banshi.

Banshi had noticed that for some time now Rashik had not asked him for any gifts of his fancy. It had hurt him more than his body aches. So at this request of Rashik's, his first instinct was to agree to it. But then he thought that it would delay Rashik's marriage. So Banshi hardened his stance and refused the loan.

Rashik told his friends that he would refuse to get married if he did not get his loan. When this news reached Banshi, he remarked that it was unheard of that the bridegroom as well as the bride would have to be paid a promised amount.

Rashik revolted openly and stopped working for Banshi. Banshi started working even harder – as if to punish himself.

The freedom movement was gathering strength and increasing the demand for hand-woven textiles. Weavers like Banshi received more orders for work. If Rashik had helped out, Banshi could have earned a lot more. But Banshi had to toil all alone, beyond the limits of his strength.

One evening, after back-breaking work the entire day, Banshi heard Rashik playing on his harmonium. He lost his temper. Rashik too shouted back. Hot and feverish, Banshi screamed out, "I have had enough of your idle ways. All you can do is ape the rich kids and play the harmonium."

With this, he tottered to his bed. But soon after, he began to regret his hot words. It seemed too cruel for him to have reproached his `little' brother like that. How could he have done it! After a while he could not bear it any more. He got up unsteadily.

Outside, Rashik was sitting silently in the dark beside his harmonium. Going up to him, Banshi took out the purse where he kept his money, and emptied it all out before Rashik.

"Take it, my little brother", he said in a choked voice, "I was saving it all for you - for you to get your bride. But I do not have the strength to go on with my saving while you mope. The money is all yours. Buy your bicycle with it - do whatever you like."

Drawing himself up, Rashik uttered a vow in a stiff voice: "Whether I have to get a bicycle or a bride, I'll do it with my own money. I will not touch yours." Without giving Banshi a chance to speak, he rushed away.

Rashik had hardly talked to Saurabhi of late. But in a few days he landed up at her place. He gave away his precious harmonium to Saurabhi's brother, and presented Saurabhi with an embroidered coverlet. Once Rashik had developed interest in embroidery and begun working on a coverlet whose pattern he had drawn out himself. It was not a run-of-the mill job, but a piece of art. Saurabhi used to watch it with a mix of patience and wonder. But just when he had almost completed the work, he lost interest in it. It was kept aside, much to Saurabhi's regret.

But in the past couple of days Rashik had completed whatever work was left. He now presented it to Saurabhi, saying: " Sairee, I have done it for you alone. Won't you take a look at it?" Saurabhi's tears began to flow. Rashik went visiting round the village, looking up everybody except his brother who lay tired and ill in bed.

Then he left the village in the dark of the winter night. Rashik had vowed to himself that he would communicate with his brother or return to his village only after he had earnt enough money to ride back on a bicycle to pay for his bride, himself.

But he found it difficult to get a job that was paying as well as fun. He tried the circus, which he had once thought so entertaining. But once he was part of the circus team, he found it rigorous and hard work. He began to pine for home. One day the owner of the circus company insulted his family profession of weaving - and Rashik left his job, empty-handed. He was ready to do the job of a `coolie', but by chance he got a job as a teacher of the craft of weaving. This was at a training centre started by young men involved in the Freedom Movement and promotion of Swadeshi goods. Rashik saved some money - but not enough to buy either the bicycle or the bride. And soon the classes began to wind up.

Rashik began to dream often of the village he had left behind, the elder brother whose affection he had spurned, and the quiet little girl he did not have the money to make his bride. Sometimes he felt like sacrificing his pride and going back to Banshi's refuge. But he did not do so. He wanted to go back with his head high - and on his own bicycle.

As luck would have it, a rich trader named Janaki Nandi happened to spot him as a prospective bridegroom for his daughter. There was some defect in his family history and he was finding it difficult to marry her off. Janaki Nandi made some enquires about Rashik's background and found that though poor, he belonged to a family that was old and respectable and higher in position than his own. He lured Rashik with a paying job and then offered him his daughter's hand in marriage.

Rashik had not received his salary for two months. The weaving classes were not working out. In that desperate state, he was quick to accept Nandi's offer.

He did not inform Banshi about his marriage. He wanted to burst upon him as a surprise, and impress him with what he had achieved. Let Banshi see how Rashik had gone ahead in life! How he had kept his vow!

At the wedding, the first item that Rashik demanded was a bicycle. It was winter again. In the gathering dusk Rashik rode his cycle along the road to his village. He wore a collared shirt, a shining black coat, a fine dhoti, colorful socks and glistening leather shoes of foreign make. He did not stop to greet anyone on the way. What he wanted was to first meet his elder brother.

By the time he reached home it had grown dark. But Rashik could see the hut had no lights on and there was a lock on the front door. A voiceless cry seemed to rise from the heart of the deserted and abandoned home: "No more, he is no more!"

As the village kids spotted him and gathered silently around him, Rashik sunk down by the door. "I know - I know - my brother is no more." A little later Saurabhi came up carrying carefully some object wrapped up in the old coverlet that Rashik had embroidered. Rashik realized it was a new bicycle.

After Rashik left home, Banshi had worked day and night unsparingly. He had saved the money for buying the bicycle as well as paying Saurabhi's father. The very day the bicycle arrived by V.P., his arms had stopped moving - his loom fell quiet.

"Wait one more year for Rashik before marrying Saurabhi off", he had pleaded with Saurabhi's father." I am paying you the promised amount of *'pan'*. And the day Rashik comes, give him this bicycle and ask him to forgive his poor brother. I could not give it to him when he had asked for it."

Rashik felt his tears choking him. He wanted to stay on in the village, working at his brother's loom and marrying the old, faithful Saurabhi. But he had already sold himself to the city and to money.

❐

12

The Return of the Young Master

Khoka Babur Pratyavartan

1

Raicharan had come from the district of Jessore in Bengal (now in Bangladesh) at the age of twelve to be a domestic servant of a Babu or gentleman in the city. He was then a slim youth with large eyes and a smooth complexion. He was a Kayastha, and so was the family of his employer. The main duty that Raicharan had was to take care of a one-year-old child.

That child was now a grown-up man, a government officer called Anukul Babu and Raicharan was still at his service.

Anukul Babu had a wife and a small child of his own. Raicharan was also married but his wife stayed at the village and they had no child as yet. Raicharan was totally devoted to the family of Anukul Babu. He was especially attached to the toddler whom he called Khoka Babu, Khoka being the Bengali word for a boy child.

From his baby days Raicharan used to rock him, fling him up in the air and catch him, sing to him and entertain him. The baby was absolutely thrilled to see Raicharan.

When the baby was old enough to crawl, Raicharan was most impressed. "Ma, your son is going to be a Judge one day", he kept telling Anukul Babu's wife, whom Raicharan called Ma as was the custom. When the baby learnt to take his first tumbling steps and call people by names such as Ma, Pichi (Pishi being paternal aunt), Raicharan was overwhelmed. The baby called him Channo (from Charan) and Raicharan could never get over that. What wonderful intelligence, he told everybody he could find.

He happily gave the toddler rides on his back, and wrestled with him, pretending to be utterly defeated every time.

Then Anukul Babu got transferred to a town on the banks of the river Padma (now in Bangladesh). Raicharan now had a new duty - taking Khoka Babu out in his perambulator or pram. Dressed in *zari*-bordered cap and satin dress, wearing gold bangles and silver anklets, Khoka Babu began to go out with Channo regularly on his drives.

Monsoon arrived. The Padma swelled up and rushed wildly along its muddy banks which often broke down under the pressure of rushing water. One cloudy day, Raicharan's tiny master - his Khoka Babu - refused to stay indoors. Raicharan had to take him out on his pram. Pushing the cart along the roadside, he went past the fields and arrived at the river bank. At one bend of the river, there stood a Kadam tree laden with flowers. Khoka Babu pointed at it and ordered, "Channo, *phu* (*phul* or flower)." Raicharan was not at all keen to wade through the mud and get to the tree. He tried to divert Khoka Babu's attention by showing him (imaginary) birds but in the end he had to give in to his demands.

"Sit quietly then in the pram while I go get the flowers", he said. "Don't you go near the waters".

He raised his *dhoti* above his knees and turning his back towards the child, walked towards the Kadam tree.But the very fact that Raicharan had asked Khoka Babu not to go near the waters, diverted the child's attention from flower to water. He got out of the pram and toddled along to the river bank. He picked up a long piece of grass and pretending it was a fishing rod, bent over the bank to fish.

There was a splash. But along the river Padma at the time of monsoon, there are such sounds all the time. Raicharan, who had climbed the tree, went on plucking the flowers. Once he got down and came back to the pram, he found it empty. He looked around. There was no one in sight. In a second his blood grew cold, "Khoka Babu! My good Khoka Babu!" he screamed out of the depths of his broken heart.

There was no reply. The river rushed by as usual. In the evening when Anukul Babu's worried wife sent people out on search, they found Raicharan screaming wildly and running around the muddy banks like a mad man.

Brought back, he slammed down at the feet of Anukul Babu's wife .To all her questions, he has just one answer, "Ma, I do not know."

Most people understood that it was the doing of the river Padma. Some suspected outsiders. But Anukul Babu's wife felt that it was Raicharan who had taken her child away for the sake of the gold and silver ornaments he had on. Anukul Babu tried to cure her of this suspicion, but failed.

2

Raicharan went back to his village in Jessore. Within a year, he had a son although he lost his wife. Raicharan felt as if it was a sin to have a son while he had let his master's son float away in the river. He hated his son and it would have died, but for the care of his sister, the baby's Pishi or paternal aunt. She called it Phelna (Bengali for a worthless something to be thrown away).

Phelna too learnt to crawl and toddle- just like Khoka Babu had done. When he cried, Raicharan felt that somewhere - in some unknown place – his Khoka Babu was feeling lost and crying out for him.

Phelna too called his Pishi as `Pichi' and hearing that, Raicharan had a strange feeling. "Khoka Babu has not been able to forget me! It is he who has taken birth in my humble hut."

He remembered the terrible suspicion Anukul Babu's wife had had. He now felt that it was somehow justified. There was no reason why he should have a son now when he had not had one for so many years. There was no explanation why his son would be crawling about, toddling around, calling out `Pichi', and showing all the signs of a future Judge – just as Khoka Babu had done. It was none other than Khoka Babu who had returned – to him!

Then onwards Raicharan was most caring and concerned towards his son. He dressed him up in *sari*-bordered caps and melted his dead wife's few ornaments to make gold bangles and silver anklets for Phelna. He did not allow any kid of the neighbourhood to play with Phelna, and himself became his constant companion and playmate. People began to laugh at the way he was treating his son as if he was the son of a Nawab or prince. But Raicharan paid no attention to them. When Phelna grew a little older, Raicharan took up a job again - in Kolkata. He lived very humbly but sent Phelna to school, and fed and clothed him in a style much above his own. He said to himself. " Khoka Babu, you are not going to suffer because you have chosen to come to your Channo."

Twelve years went by. Raicharan's son had grown up into a good-looking and healthy youth with a taste for stylish clothes and comfortable living. Raicharan had kept it a secret that he was Phelna's father. So Phelna's friends sometimes made gentle fun of Raicharan who was a country bumpkin to them. Phelna did love his father, but in a condescending way. Raicharan himself did not behave to him exactly like a father. He seemed rather to be serving him.

Raicharan was growing old. He had sold off whatever little property he had had in the village, and that money too was running out. Phelna had begun to complain about the food and clothes Raicharan could provide for him.

3

Raicharan suddenly gave up his job and went to the small town where Anukul Babu was then posted.

Anukul Babu had not had a second child. His wife was still nurturing her grief in her bosom. She hankered for a child and wasted money on herbs and cures that promised to make her a mother again. Anukul Babu was moved to see Raicharan grown so old. He made a thousand enquiries about his present condition and wanted to re-employ him.

All Raicharan wanted was to see `Ma' again. Anukul Babu's wife did not look pleased to see Raicharan. But Raicharan ignored that and said to her with folded palms: "Ma, it was indeed I who had stolen your son. It was not Padma or anyone else. It was I - ungrateful and unworthy".

"What are you saying?" Anukul Babu spoke out, shocked. "Where is he?"

"He is with me and I will bring him the day after tomorrow."

The day after, a Sunday, Anukul Babu and his wife waited impatiently for Raicharan, and he did turn up - with Phelna.

Anukul Babu's wife asked no questions, made no queries,

but simply took Phelna on her lap. Laughing and crying, gazing into his eyes, smelling his forehead, she was beyond herself with joy. Anukul Babu too felt affection surging up in his bosom. Indeed, there was a pleasant-looking youth before them, with no signs of a poor upbringing on him. Even then Anukul Babu asked, "Is there any proof?"

"Is there ever a proof of such black deeds? God alone knows that I stole your son. No one on earth does."

Anukul Babu decided that it was not advisable to be finicky about proofs when his wife had accepted the youth so wholeheartedly. Besides, where would poor Raicharan get such a youth and why should he unnecessarily trick him?"

Talking to the youth, he discovered that he had been staying with Raicharan from his childhood but Raicharan had never behaved exactly like his father with him, but more like his servant. Thrusting away all suspicion from his mind, Anukul Babu said: "But Raicharan, you must never come anywhere near us again."

Folding his palms, in a thick, choked voice Raicharan said, "Master, where will I go at this age?"

"Let him stay", said Anukul Babu's wife. "I forgive him."

A stickler for what is correct, Anukul Babu said, "His offense is not fit to be forgiven."

"It was not I who committed that offense."

"Who was it then?"

"My fate!"

But such an explanation does not satisfy any educated person. Anukul Babu refused to show mercy.

"I don't have anyone else in the world", pleaded Raicharan.

Phelna had by now gathered that he was the son of a

prominent government official. Raicharan had stolen him and brought him up as his son – which was an insult. He felt somewhat angry but said in a generous manner to Anukul Babu, "Baba (father), forgive him. If you do not let him stay in the house, at least send him some money every month."

After this, Raicharan did not say a single word. He gazed into his son's face one last time, touched everyone's feet, and went out. He got mixed and lost in the vast population of the earth. When at the end of the month Anukul Babu sent money at his village address, it came back. No one by that name lived there any more.

❐

13

The Vendor from Kabul

Kabuliwala

Ever since my five-year-old Mini has learnt to speak, she has created a problem. She cannot stop talking even for a moment. Not a moment does she waste in silence. Her mother often scolded her in order to shut her up. But although I was a busy man working on a novel, I never had the heart to do so. So Mini would always come to me with her queries and there would ensue lively discussions between us.

One day I was at a stage of writing when my hero and heroine were in a situation of the greatest suspense. Just then Mini came rushing in.

"Father, our gatekeeper is stupid. He calls a *kak* (Bengali for crow) a *kaua* (Hindi equivalent)".

What could I as her father do? How could I explain to her the concept of the various languages that exist in this world? But even before I could decide on where to start, Mini had already started off on another subject altogether.

"Bhola was telling me how it rains... He told me that there is a huge elephant hidden behind the clouds. It fills its trunk with water and pours it over us. That is how we have the rains. Isn't Bhola clever, father?"

Before I had the time to think about a suitable reply, there came another question.

"Father, what is mother to you?"

To this I could only reply: "Go out and play Mini, I have work to do." But Mini just sat down below my desk in front of a window from which one could see the road, and started to play an imaginary game. Suddenly she left her game and turned towards the window. "Kabuliwala! O Kabuliwala!" she started yelling.

I too looked out to see a huge and hefty 'Kabuliwala' (One who is from Kabul) walk slowly by. He was wearing the usual loose dress and a turban that men from Afghanistan usually wore. There was a huge *thaila* or sack on his back and a few boxes of grapes in one hand.

Just as I feared, the Kabuliwala heard her call and turned around to see where the cry was coming from. But the minute she saw the Kabuliwala's face, Mini turned around and was off to hide – maybe she believed that the sack that the Kabuliwala carried held some live children like her. I knew that now there would be no way in which my novel could be completed and sure enough, within a few seconds, the Kabuliwala was standing there at the gate, smiling and saluting.

I knew that the only way in which I could get on with my work was to buy something from the man and send him away. So, I went up to the Kabuliwala and bought some dry fruits, but soon I found myself in a conversation with him, chatting about the Russians, the English and also about other policies of the government.

Eventually, when it was time for the Kabuliwala to leave, he turned to me and said, "Babu, where is that *khonkhi* (little girl)?"

I knew that he had to get my little daughter get over her fear of Kabuliwalas and therefore he called out to her.

Mini did come out, but she clung on to me, refusing to come any closer to the Kabuliwala. He offered her some nuts and raisins, but Mini hung back. That was how their first meeting went.

After a few days, one morning when I was about to leave the house, I was surprised to see Mini and the Kabuliwala sitting in the courtyard and chatting. Mini was laughing and talking and the Kabuliwala was responding in broken Bengali. It seemed to me that in all the five years of her life, she had never got a listener more patient than the man from Afganistan - other than myself, of course!

I saw that the corner of her small *sari* was stuffed with all sorts of dry fruits and nuts. I handed an eight-anna piece to the Kabuliwala, saying: "Why are you giving her all these?" The Kabuliwala seemed to accept the money, but later Mini's mother found out that he had quietly given it back to Mini.

The Kabuliwala began to come almost every day and bribe Mini with his gifts of nuts and raisins. Soon Mini lost her fear and the two of them became the best of friends. I would hear them talk for hours. There were a few standard jokes that they exchanged regularly.

Mini would ask her new-found friend, "Kabuliwala, what do you have in your sack?"

The Kabuliwala would add a nasal twang to his voice and reply, "*Hanthi,* an elephant, *khonkhi.*"

Again, the Kabuliwala would often ask: "*Khonkhi,* won't you ever be going to your *sasurbari* (father-in-law's house)?"

Unlike most Bengali girls of her age, Mini did not exactly

know what marriage and going to one's *sasurbari* meant. Being somewhat modern in outlook, her mother and I had not yet made her wise as to it. But Mini did not let Kabuliwala see that she was out of her depth. She countered his query with: "Well, what about you? Will **you** be going there?"

Now the word *sasur-bari* or 'father-in-law's place' is slang for 'jail' because both are places where one can stay free of cost. So the minute Mini asked the question, the Kabuliwala replied, "*Hami sasur ke marbe*(I will beat up my father-in-law)!" Mini went into peals of laughter imagining the predicament of an unknown creature named *sasur*.

While I took great pleasure in seeing the Kabuliwala and my daughter have their chats, her mother was scared that he would one day kidnap her daughter and sell her off to Afghanistan. Nevertheless Mini and the Kabuliwala's friendship kept growing over the months.

Soon it was January and it was time for the Kabuliwala to go back home. This was the period when he would go to all his debtors and start collecting their debts. Though this was a pretty busy time for him, he would still manage to find the time to come and meet Mini some time in the day. If he was unable to come during the day, he would surely pay her a visit in the evening.

A few days later, I was busy writing at my desk when suddenly I heard a row from the streets. I looked out and saw the Kabuliwala, with his hands tied up, being dragged away by two policemen. I rushed out to know what was happening. When I reached the three men, I could see that the Kabuliwala's shirtfront was bloodstained and that one of the policemen was carrying a bloodied knife. "This Kabuliwala claims", said the policeman, "that he had sold a rug to a man in this locality. But when he pressed him for the payment, the man denied the entire deal. So in a mad rage, the Kabuliwala has stabbed the man."

Just as I was wondering as to what could be done, Mini came running out with her usual "Kabuliwala! O Kabuliwala," only to see him handcuffed and without his sack of elephants on his back. In a tone of amusement, she asked, "Where are you going, Kabuliwala, to your father-in-law's house?"

At these words, the Kabuliwala's face lit up and he replied, "Yes, little one, I am going to meet my father-in-law. I would have given him a sound thrashing, but alas, my hands are tied."

Mini broke into laughter as the Kabuliwala was dragged away by the policemen. I heard later that he was convicted of his crime and sent to jail.

Time passed and the Kabuliwala was slowly forgotten. Mini was growing up and now she began spending more time with girls. She did not come to my room as often as she used to.

Soon it was time for her marriage. Her mother and I got busy with the preparations. On the day of the actual wedding, I was busy looking into the details, when a man suddenly presented himself before me. I turned around to see that it was the Kabuliwala. He no longer had his sack, and his old look of strength. "How are you?" I asked. "It has been a long time since I last saw you."

"I was released from jail yesterday," said the Kabuliwala, smiling.

These words struck me like a blow. I had never met a person who had been sent to jail for committing a crime. I suddenly found myself wishing that the Kabuliwala had not come today, of all the days, the auspicious day of my daughter's marriage.

"I see," I hurriedly replied. "We are very busy today, can you come and meet me some other time?"

The Kabuliwala did not look very disappointed. What he said was: "May I see your daughter once before I go?"

I realized that the Kabuliwala had perhaps not realized that Mini had grown up in all these years. Did he expect the child he knew to come running out and greet him in her usual way? However I remembered that I had to get the man out of my house and said, "Everyone is very busy today. Come back some other time!"

Now the Kabuliwala turned sadly away. The disappointment on the face of such a huge man made me feel very sorry for him. Just as I was about to ask him to come back, I saw that the Kabuliwala was coming back on his own.

"I will come back some other day to meet you, Babuji, but could you please give this to your little child?" he asked as he took out a small bag of dry fruits. He had obviously got it especially for Mini. I immediately took out some money and was about to hand it over to the Kabuliwala, when he stopped me, "No, Babu, no. I do want any money. You see, back in Afghanistan I too have a little girl like yours. It is remembering her face that I come here to give your daughter some nuts. I do not come here to make sales."

He brought out a small and crumpled piece of paper from the front of his loose, flowing robe. Most carefully he spread it out on the table before me.

I saw that on the paper there was the imprint of a small palm. It was not a photograph or oil painting. A child's hand had been anointed with ink and pressed palm down on the paper. It had made a mark - a mark of remembrance - a memento - and that's what the Kabuliwala had kept next to his chest when he sold his nuts in a land so far away from his home. A small palm print had kept the heart inside his huge body soft and alive.

I felt tears filling my eyes. I forgot the difference in the positions of the Kabuliwala and myself. All I could think of was that the Kabuliwala too was a father like me. I sent word inside to send Mini out to meet the Kabuliwala. Mini's mother objected from within the house but I paid no heed.

Finally, Mini arrived. Seeing her all grown up and dressed as a bride, the Kabuliwala was a little taken aback but tried to joke like before: "*Khonkhi*, I see that you are now going to your *sasurbari*!"

Mini now knew what the Kabuliwala meant and turned away shyly and silently. The old joke did not work any more. Perhaps it dawned on the Kabuliwala that his daughter too must have grown up and he would have to start making friends with her all over again. And who knows what had happened to her in all this while. As Mini walked off, the huge Kabuliwala sat down on the floor with a big sigh.

I gave him some money. "With this, go back home to your daughter", I advised. "Your joy at seeing your daughter again will bring blessings upon my daughter."

Giving that money to the Kabuliwala meant that I had to strike off some of the planned heads of wedding expenditure such as lighting and band. Mini's mother was not too happy at this. But I knew that the blessings of another father would make my daughter's wedding brighter.

❐

14

Wish-fulfillment

Ichchhapuran

Subalchandra's son was named Sushilchandra. But a person is not always like his name. So Su-bal(strength) was somewhat weak and Su-shil(polite) was not a very quiet chap.

The son, that is Sushil, pestered everyone in the neighbourhood. His father, that is, Subal, often chased after him in order to reprimand. But he had arthritis while his son could run like the deer. So the blows did not always fall in the right places. But the days when Sushil got caught, he received no mercy.

On this Saturday, school was coming to an end at 2 in the afternoon. But Sushil did not in the least feel like going to school today. He had a geography test today; besides the Bose family in the neighbourhood was having a show of fireworks in the late evening. Sushil wanted to spend his day there watching the preparations.

After a lot of thinking, he went and lay down on the bed when the time came for going to school. His father came up and asked, "What's wrong, aren't you going to school today?"

"I have a stomach-ache", answered Sushil. "I will not be able to go to school today."

Subal saw through his excuse. He decided to teach him a lesson." Stomach-ache? Well then, no need to go out anywhere. There will be fireworks at the Boses', but I will not send you there. I had got some lozenges for you. But no need for you to have them today! Quietly lie down on your bed. I will get you some *panchan* (herbal concoction with a bitter taste)."

He latched up the door from outside. Sushil was appalled. He loved lozenges as much as he hated *panchan*. And he had been dying to see the fireworks at the Boses'!

As Subal-babu entered with a huge bowl of bitter herbal juice, Sushil got out of the bed with alacrity.

"My stomach-ache is absolutely gone. I'll be going to school today."

"No need of that. You just take this and have some rest". With this, Sushil forced down the bitter juice down Sushil's throat and went away, locking the door from outside.

Sushil lay on the bed all day, weeping. "If only I could be as old as Baba(father), I could do as I like, and no one would be able to stop me."

Subal-babu himself sat outside thinking: 'my parents were too lenient with me. That is why I did not get much schooling in my childhood. If only I could get my childhood back, I would not waste my time but only devote myself to my incomplete education.'

Ichha-thakrun (the presiding deity of wish-fulfillment) was passing by. She divined their thoughts. "Well, let us see what comes of my fulfilling their wishes for a while."

She went up to the father and said, "Your wish will come true. From tomorrow you will be your son's age."

To the son she said, "From tomorrow you will be as old as your father".

Both father and son were thrilled at this.

Old Subal had a problem with his sleep. Only in the early hours of dawn could he catch some sound sleep. But the next morning, he got up very early and jumped out of the bed. He saw that he had indeed become very young. The teeth that he had lost to age had sprung up again. His beard and whiskers had vanished. The *kurta* that he had gone to sleep in had become loose that the sleeves were reaching down to the ground and the neck had fallen to the chest. The pleats of the dhoti had become so long that it was difficult to take steps.

Our Sushil - who used to get up early and create mischief all around - found it difficult to get up from his sleep today. When finally his father Subal's shouts and yells woke him up, he discovered that his clothing had become so tight that they were about to burst into pieces. His entire body had grown in size. Beard and whiskers covered half the face, and instead of his thick crop of hair, there was shining baldness at front.

He hardly felt like getting out of his bed this morning. He yawned and turned over several times before he left the bed out of sheer irritation at the noise his father Sushilchandra was making.

Both of them had their wishes fulfilled, but there arose a huge problem.

Sushil used to think that if he were old and independent like his father, he would do as he liked - climbing trees, diving, eating green mangoes, taking baby birds down from the nests and roaming everywhere. He would come and go as he liked without anyone to check him. But the strange thing was that on this morning he had absolutely no desire to climb up a tree. Looking at the pond overgrown with moss and fronds, he felt he would be shivering with fever if he took a dip in it. He sat on a mat, quietly turning various ideas in his mind. Once he felt that it was not a good idea to give up sports and outdoor activities altogether. He tried to climb up a fruit tree nearby. But the very tree he had climbed yesterday like a squirrel proved insurmountable to his aged body. As soon as he had caught on to a lower branch, it broke under his weight and Sushil fell down on the ground. Passers by laughed their head off to see an old man trying to act like a kid and failing. Shamefacedly Sushil returned to his mat, and asked the servant to get him some lozenges from the market.

Sushil had a weakness for lozenges. Whatever small coins he could get, he spent on the multi-colored lozenges sold in the shop next to his school. He dreamt of days when he would have money like his father did, he would buy pockets full of lozenges. Today when the servant brought a whole rupee's worth of lozenges, he put one into his mouth, but it did not taste good at all, in the toothless mouth of an old man. He thought of giving them away to son Subal but refrained, fearing that they might upset his stomach.

Kids who had till yesterday played `ha-do-do'( Bengali variety of the boisterous game `hu-tu-tu') with Sushil, came to his house looking for him. They ran away on seeing the aged Sushil and Sushil too felt that they would create a racket and disturb the quiet reverie he was enjoying.

Earlier, sitting on his mat and brooding over the past, Subal Chandra had often thought that he would devote his energies to studies if ever he got a second chance. But now he hardly felt like going to school. Sushil used to come up and ask, "Baba, aren't you going to school today?" Subal used to scratch his head and mumble, "My stomach is aching ..". "I know all about such stomach-aches; I have had many of them when I had to go to school", Sushil used to say angrily.

Actually Sushil had been so good at avoiding going to school that it was difficult for Subal to trick him. Sushil began to force his tiny father to go to school. On coming back from school, Subal wanted to run around playing. But Sushil made him sit down to work out long and difficult sums. To have his game of chess in peace with his cronies, Sushil arranged a private tutor to keep Subal quiet in the evenings ---going on till ten in the night.

Sushil was extremely strict about food to be served to his father, whom he remembered to have problems of acidity whenever he over-ate. But on suddenly becoming a kid, Subal had got an excellent digestive system. With the meager amounts that he got now, he went hungry all day. As he became skin and bones, Sushil began to pour more and more medicine down his throat.

Sushil himself too had problems. He could no longer carry off what he attempted according to his old habits. Earlier, he made it a point to go and watch every *jatra* (open air village play performance) in every sort of weather. Now he caught a cold doing so, and was laid up in bed for three weeks with fever and body-ache. Bathing in the pond in the old, accustomed way brought on rheumatoid arthritis treatment of which took six months. Since then he bathed only at the interval of two days and in hot water. In fact, he did not let Subal use the pond. Unmindful of the present, he sometimes jumped down from the bed and his very bones protested. He stuffed *paan* into his mouth only to realize that he had no teeth to chew the betel-leaf with. He applied the brush and comb to his head only to remember that it was almost entirely bald. Earlier he used to tease an old lady in the village by throwing stones at her water-pot. Sometimes he did so now by the force of sheer habit. On seeing a senior person indulge in childish pranks, people use to chase him away and he used to hide his face in shame.

Subalchandra too sometimes forgot that he was now a child. He used to join the group of village elders, nod his head and comment on issues just like them. They used to box his hears and say: "Get lost and don't act precocious!" He used to walk up to his teacher at school, and ask for a puff at the *hukkah* (old-fashioned equipment for smoking). The teacher used to make him stand up on the bench on one leg. One day he walked up to the barber and asked, "You fellow, why haven't you come since long for shaving me?" Taking it for a joke, the barber answered back: "I'll be coming after a decade or so." Sometimes, out of old habit, he used to go and smack Sushil. Sushil used to scream out: "Is this what you are learning at school-- raising your hands against senior people?" People used to rush up from all sides and rain blows upon Subal.

Then Subal began to pray: "If only I could become old like my son Sushil – old and independent!"

Sushil too prayed everyday with folded palms: "O God! Make me young like my father so that I can happily play about. Baba has become so mischievous that I cannot keep him in check. I am getting frantic with worry."

Ichha-thakurani, the deity of wish-fulfillment, now came up to them and asked, "So, have you had enough of your fancies?"

"Yes", both of them bowed deeply to the deity. "We have had enough. Now kindly let us go back to what we were."

"Alright", said the deity of wishes, "that is what will happen when you get up tomorrow."

The next day Subal woke up an aged man as he used to be and Sushil woke up - a kid. Both of them felt as if they had just come out of a dream. Subal asked in a thick voice, "Sushil, aren't you going to memorize your grammar lesson?"

Scratching his head, Sushil said, "Baba, I have lost my grammar book."

❐

15

Robbed of the Gem

Monihara

My boat was tied to the crumbling embankment of the river.

The sun had just set. The boatman was busy reading his *namaz* from the rooftop of the boat. The palatial building next to the river bank was in ruins — the doors and windows and even the balconies of the building were falling apart. I was quietly sitting on the steps that led down to the river and tears were about to come into my dry eyes, when a voice pierced the silence and shocked me.

"Where are you from, Sir?"

The man who asked me the question was sitting at the top of the stairs. The condition of his clothes did speak a great deal about his poverty. He may have walked in after his day's work and having no money to buy an evening snack, must have decided to taken in whiffs of the river air as refreshment.

"I am from Ranchi", I replied.

"And your name, Sir?"

I gave a name, but it was not mine.

"What brings you here?"

"A change of scene".

"Where are you staying?"

I pointed to the ruined mansion. He must have thought that I was hunting for some treasures in there. He turned out to be the local school teacher whose appearance reminded me a lot Coleridge's Ancient Mariner. He wanted to narrate to me a tragic tale that had occurred fifteen years ago, in the very mansion which stood in ruins upon the riverside.

The boatman had finished offering prayers and got down to cooking his meal. The light on the horizon was fading out, the play of the soft sun-rays giving the palace a ghostly look.

The school master began....

* *

Almost ten years before I came to this village, the beautiful, college educated Monimalika and her husband, the well-meaning, city bred Phanibhushan Saha used to live in this house. Phanibhushan had inherited his father's palatial house and the family business. He and Monimalika had no children and Phanibhushan was very much in love with his wife. He showered her with gifts comprising of the best of Dhakai saris and jewelry. Monimalika, however, had presumed that it was her birthright to get the gifts. She was always in the mood to receive, never to reciprocate. Not even with love.

Monimalika kept to herself in the house and did not like socializing with the local people. Phanibhushan remained busy throughout the day with affairs of his business.

Unfortunately, Phanibhushan's business had slowly moved in to major losses and there came a time when he needed an urgent funding of almost one and a half lakh of rupees. He had to arrange for the money within five days to save his business from the crisis. Phanibhushan did not support the idea of approaching the local moneylenders for he feared that if the word of his borrowing went around, it would further affect his business adversely. He thought it would be easier to mortgage some valuable item like jewelry and obtain a loan as it would involve very little paper work. He approached Monimalika and suggested that she part with her ornaments so that Phanibhushan could quickly organize the funds and save the business from sinking. Monimalika heard him out but did not respond either way. Phanibhushan got the message and though saddened by his wife's reaction, he left for Kolkata in order to try and secure the funds by some other means.

Next day, Monimalika sent for Madhusudan, her cousin, who did a small job in her husband's office. She asked him for advice, which was immediately offered as Madhusudan saw a game plan for himself.

"I don't think he will ever be able to secure the money. The amount he is looking for is big. Ultimately, he will be forced to return and pawn your ornaments," he warned.

Monimalika shuddered at the very thought of having to take off all her ornaments from her hands and body and exchange them for money to save the business.

"What shall I do?" she asked Madhusudan.

"Let us leave right away and go to your parent's house," he suggested. He was sure to ultimately lay his hands on a better part of the ornaments.

Monimalika immediately agreed and told Madhusudan to arrange for a boat. In the evening a boat arrived at the banks of the river. At the crack of dawn, wrapped in a shawl from head to toe, Monimalika got on to the boat.

Once the boat left the banks and sped away with the torrent, the shrewd Madhusudan asked her to hand over the jewelry box to him for safe keeping. As Monimalika would not trust anybody with the box, she had, piece by piece, worn every item of jewelry she possessed. She was scared that in case she ever parted with the box, she would be ruined. She may not have understood her husband Phanibhushan, but was certainly correct in her assessment about her cousin Madhusudan.

Before leaving, Madhusudan had left a note for Phanibhushan's office manager that he would be escorting Monimalika to her parents' house. The next day when the manager read the note, he informed Phanibhushan about his wife's departure and also added that Phanibhushan was, perhaps, not right in permitting his wife to indulge to this extent.

Phanibhushan was shocked to hear the news. He had not taken and pawned his wife's jewelry. He had come to Kolkata to try and raise the funds on his own. Then, why did his wife not trust him with the ornaments, he wondered.

Accepting his fate, he decided to complete his business and then return home. He expected that after having left the jewelry box at her father's house, Monimalika would have returned home. To his dismay, on his return, he found the door locked. Breaking open the door, he found that the trunk containing the ornaments was empty.

The old caretaker suggested that without losing any further time, they should look for Monimalika, and accordingly, a search operation was carried out. All boats, boat men, river ways...everything was looked in to, and everyone was interrogated, but there was no sign of Monimalika. Meanwhile, the messenger who was sent to Monimalika's village returned with the news that she had not reached there.

Giving up all hopes to find Monimalika, Phanibhushan walked in to the empty room. Everything in the room was in position as before...the decanter, the Chinese doll, the small bottles of essence...only the lady was not present.

Late in the night the torrential rains had finally stopped. The *Jatra* being performed in the village had also come to an end. The music had stopped. The air was heavy as a morose Phanibhushan reclined in the empty room, pining for Monimalika to suddenly enter and light up the house — and his life.

Suddenly, he heard a metallic noise in the darkness. It was slowly coming up the stairs that led to the bank of the river. He sat up with an air of excitement. The noise was moving up to the main entrance of the house. The main door had been locked by the *durwan*. There was a sound of violent knocking on the door. The noise was that of heavy ornaments banging against each other.

Phanibhushan ran out of the room, down the stairs and reached the main door. He was sweating and his body was cold like ice. He opened the door, but he found nobody there.

Next day he asked the *durwan* to keep the door open. The *durwan* protested saying there was another *jatra* performance slated that night and it would not be safe or wise to keep the main door unlocked. He offered to stay up the whole night instead. Phanibhushan declined his offer and insisted that he too attend the *jatra* performance that night and leave him alone in the mansion. The absurd instruction baffled the *durwan*.

That night, again there was the noise moving up the stairs

from the bank. The sound got closer and reached the edge of the door to the room. His heart beating, Phanibhushan yelled, "Moni!" There was silence.

The following night Phanibhushan announced that he wanted, again, to spend the night all by himself. His staff thought that the master may be practicing some voodoo activity. He maintained a fast all day.

Night fell. Like the previous two nights, the heavy sound of ornaments started moving up the stairs. As Phanibhushan waited with bated breath and closed eyes, the sound entered the room and moved past the lamp, the almirah, in fact every point in the room, and finally stopped very close to Phanibhushan.

He gradually opened his eyes and to his utter shock, he found a full skeleton standing in front of him! The skeleton wore eight rings in eight fingers, bangles, necklace…in fact the bones were all draped with sparkling ornaments.

His blood froze…horrified, he tried to close his eyes but, failed. The skeleton quietly pointed at Phanibhushan and signaled him to follow her. He did likewise, and the skeleton led him to the balcony, on to the main doorway and out to the stairs leading to the bank. Phanibhushan was totally mesmerized and followed without any second thoughts. The river was flowing, gushing and gurgling as it did so – the skeleton stepped in to the turbulent waters of the river…Phanibhushan followed, and as he did so, he was instantly swept away by the strong current. He offered no resistance, and despite being a swimmer, did not even attempt to stay afloat.

* *

The school master stopped. I had not said a word till now.

"I don't think you believed this story?' he asked me.

"Did you?" it was my turn to ask him now.

"Not really. First, I don't think God Almighty is a novelist – He has many other urgent missions to attend to and…"

"…and secondly, I myself am Phanibhushan Saha", I interrupted.

The school master was not in the least ashamed. "I guessed right. What was your wife's name?"

"Nrityakali", I replied.

❒

16

The Hidden Treasure

Guptadhan

It was a moonless night. Mrityunjaya sat in a small temple within the courtyard of his ancestral house. In the temple there stood the idol of Kali, his family deity. Throughout the night he worshipped the idol according to *tantrik* rituals.

It was dawn by the time he finished.

Now he moved away the mat on which the idol was placed, and took out a wooden box from underneath. He opened it with a key attached to his *upavita* string. As soon as he opened it, he gave a start and hit his forehead with his hand in a gesture of despair.

It was empty. Mrityunjaya looked everywhere – around the idol, around the temple, all though the night.

In the morning, he sat down utterly fatigued, he found a *sanyasi* or mendicant with matted hair standing right in front.

As Mrityunjaya bowed to him, the mendicant blessed him. "You are grieving uselessly, my child".

Surprised, Mrityunjaya blurted out:" You are omniscient! How else did you know that I was grieving? I hadn't said a word to anyone."

"I tell you, my child, do not grieve for what you have lost, but celebrate!"

"You know everything, then!" Mrityunjaya hugged the mendicant's feet. "Tell me how to get it back. Or I won't let you go."

The whole day he served the mendicant in every way he could. But next morning he found the mendicant gone.

2

When Mrityunjaya was but a child, a mendicant had come just like this and stood before his grandfather Harihara.

Harihara hosted him for several days and served him so well that the mendicant asked if he could do anything for him.

"If you are pleased with me, make our family wealthy and prosperous again - richer than our other relatives".

The mendicant smiled a little. "Why try to be richer than all others? Stay the way you are and be happy."

But Harihara would not let him go. He was ready to do anything to make his family powerful and prosperous – prove its superiority over that of his relatives.

Then the mendicant took out a roll of thick, rough paper wrapped in cloth. As he unfurled it, Harihara saw that it had various symbols arranged within various circular shapes. At the end there was a rhyme:

Paye dhorey sadha

Ra nahi day Radha

(Radha does not give *dha* although I plead, touching her feet, *pa*).

Sheshey dilo ra

Pagol chharo pa

(In the end she did give *ra* or response: *pagol*, mad fellow! Let go of my feet!")

Tentul bater koley koley

Dokkhine jao choley

(The Tamarind on the lap of the Banyan - go south!)

Ishankoney Ishani

Koye dilam nishani

(Durga in the north-west,

Now I have given you the clue!)

"But I cannot made any sense of it, Baba ", said Harihara.

"Keep it with you. Worship the goddess Kali. By her favour someone or the other will be able to decipher this writing. Then he will acquire wealth that is beyond compare in this world."

"O Baba, will you not explain it to me?" pleaded Harihara.

"No", said the mendicant. "You have to strive to decipher it -you have to do it yourself."

Just then Shankara, Harihara's younger brother, came up. As soon as he saw him, Harihara quickly tried to hide the scroll.

"The trouble with being superior has started already!" smiled the mendicant. "But there is no need to hide it or keep it secret. Only one person will be able to penetrate through to its secret. Try as they might, no one else will be able to do so. Now out of you that special person will be, nobody knows. So you can easily keep it in everybody's sight."

The mendicant went away. But in spite of what he had said, Harihara could not keep it out in the open. So that his younger brother Shankara cannot get to it, so that no one else, in fact, can benefit from it, he kept it locked up in a wooden box under the seat of their family deity Kali. Every moonless night, that is, every fortnight, he worshipped the deity and at midnight, opened the box, took out the scroll, in the hope that the deity would bless him with the power to decipher it."

Shankara began to pester Harihara to let him have a look at the scroll." I have burnt it up", Harihara told him. "It was only some stuff and nonsense that fraud of a mendicant fooled me with."

Shankara was silent. Then after a couple of days he just vanished from the place.

Harihara could think of nothing but the hidden treasure, and became incapable of any other work. Just before his death, he passed this scroll on to his son. On inheriting the scroll, the son gave up working and spent his entire life worshipping Kali and studying the scroll.

On his death, the scroll had gone to his son - Mrityunjaya, and as his financial conditions became worse, he became more and more engrossed in the scroll, putting his entire mind into it.

It was at this stage that – on one moonless night – the scroll could no longer be found, and the mendicant who had come also disappeared.

"I cannot let him go", said Mrityunjaya. "He is the one who holds all the clues to the hidden treasure".

He left home in search of the vanished mendicant. One whole year passed by with him on the roads.

3

The village was called Dharagol. Mrityunjaya was sitting at a grocery shop having a smoke. Suddenly he caught sight of a mendicant walking across the field to the forest adjoining the village. By the time it struck him that it was the very mendicant he was looking for; the mendicant who had visited his home and made off with the scroll. The grocer told Mrityunjaya that the forest had in epic times been a prosperous town. Epidemics had destroyed it, but it was rumored that it contained hidden treasure. But no one dared to look for it, even in broad daylight. Those who had done so had never returned.

Mrityunjaya was spending the night in the grocer's shop. As he lay tossing and turning, fending of swarms of mosquitoes, the rhyme he by now knew by heart came back to him again and again:

Radha does not give dha although I plead, touching her feet.

In the end she did give *ra* or response: mad fellow! Let go of my feet!"

As he dozed off in the early hours of the dawn, they suddenly became clear in the easiest of ways.

If Radha does not give ra, there remains only dha.

If she gives ra in the end, it becomes ra after dha or dha-ra.

If pagol (mad fellow) lets go of her feet (pa), what remains is gol.

That makes it dha-ra-gol, and the village was indeed named Dharagol!

Mrityunjaya jumped out of his sleep.

4

The whole of next day he spent in the jungle, finding his way out with great difficulty, and returning tired and hungry in the evening. He went in again the next morning taking some puffed rice with him.

Struggling through the jungle all day, in the afternoon, he came upon a Tamarind tree around which a huge Banyan had taken root.

Immediately he remembered the lines:

The Tamarind on the lap of the Banyan – go south!

Going south he came upon an impenetrable growth of cane. As he turned back, through the branches of the Banyan-Tamarind, he caught sight of the spire of a temple.

Finding his way to the ruined temple, he found traces of a recent fire before it, along with a mendicant's saffron robe, blanket and water-pot.

In the gathering darkness, Mrityunjaya saw a slab of stone that had broken and fallen off from the temple. There were some etchings on it – the same circular arrangement of letters and symbols that had been there on the scroll! Mrityunjaya had seen it so many times as he had bent over it in the lamplight after worshipping Kali at his own home.

That meant that he was close upon the treasure! Mrityunjaya began to tremble with excitement.

As the night fell, he saw firelight in the distance among the trees.

He advanced and saw that it was the mendicant – the one that had visited his home.

In front of him was spread out the familiar scroll. No wonder he had asked Mrityunjaya not to grieve for it. He had stolen it himself!

What he was doing was to study it, make calculations, scratch upon the forest floor with a stick, realize he had miscalculated, nod his head in despair, and start calculating once again. He gave up his efforts at dawn and Mrityunjaya too carefully got out of the forest. Next day he was quite late in going back. It was night already and he could not find his way to wherever the mendicant was. But he had decided that he just **had to** find him. He alone could guide him to the treasure. Day after day he persisted in coming to the forest at night in search of the mendicant.

6

Making mistakes again and again, the mendicant finally discovered a tunnel. With a flare in his hand, he entered the tunnel. It was damp inside, with frogs lying in a heap on the slimy wall. The mendicant came some distance and then found him face to face with a blank wall. A dead end.

He came out and again sat before the scroll, thinking. That night, following certain instructions he had deciphered, he removed a brick from that blank wall and found another tunnel that branched off.

He crawled along it and found it to come to another blank wall. He came the next day with fresh instructions that he had again deciphered and found a further tunnel branching off. This went on till the fifth night. "I cannot go wrong tonight!" said the mendicant as he entered the tunnel on this fifth night.

Creeping along an intricate network of passages, carefully carrying his flare, he came upon a room that was round in shape and had a deep well at the centre of it. A thick iron chain attached to the roof went down into the well. With a great effort, the mendicant shook it a little. Down somewhere in the hollow of the well, it fit something with a clang. The metallic sound rose up from the depths and echoed round and round the room. "I have got it!" shouted out the mendicant.

Instantly there rolled out a rock from somewhere in the darkness of that room, and something live fell down and screamed out in pain.

7

"Why, it is Mrityunjaya!" exclaimed the mendicant.

"Fraud! Cheat! ", Mrityunjaya said wildly and painfull. " You stole my scroll - a mendicant had given it to my grandfather and said that only a member of our family will be able to decipher it. The hidden treasure it leads to thus belongs to me and my family alone. That is why I have been after you all this time. Weakened as I am by hunger, I have been following you through the tunnels. Finally, when just now you said, "Got it!" I could not stop myself from throwing that rock at you. But instead of killing you, I just hurt myself. I think I have broken my leg. But I curse you. That hidden treasure is mine. My ancestors have died thinking of it. Our family has grown impoverished dreaming of it. I have left my wife and child at home and been roaming here and there like a mad man - hankering for it. You can't take it away from right under my nose!"

8

"Then listen, Mrityunjaya. I am none other than your grandfather's younger brother Shankara, who had left home long back."

A huge sigh came out of Mrityunjaya.

This meant that the mendicant, belonging to the same family, did have a claim upon the hidden treasure. It was not that Mriytunjaya alone had a right to it.

Shankara - the mendicant who was his grand-uncle - told him his story.

When he realized that elder brother Harihara was not going to let him have a look at the scroll, Shankara had found out where her was hiding it. He made a duplicate key to the wooden box at the feet their family deity Kali. Opening it secretly for some time every day, he painstakingly made a copy of the scroll. Then he left home in search for the hidden treasure. Year after year he tried to make out the secret of the scroll. He kept the company of mendicants in the hope that one of them will help him. None could. A couple of false mendicants even tried to steal the scroll away from him. Then in Kumaon hills he came in contact with a Swamiji who cured him of his mad craving for the hidden treasure. He lost his desire for wealth and even burnt up the scroll. Taking pleasure in the beauties of nature, he moved about now with a true mendicant's spirit.

In course of those travels, he just happened to come to this area and as he took shelter in the ruined temple in the jungle, he chanced upon stone slabs lying here and there with signs and symbols that had been there in the scroll.

He understood that he was within reach of what he had been after for so long. But he no longer had any desire for wealth or good living. He felt he should just move away, leaving the treasure hidden where it was. But then he was curious as well, and wanted to get to the bottom of the mystery - where *was* the treasure hidden? He began to regret destroying the scroll containing the clues. Gradually the desire to solve this problem grew so strong that he went down to his old village and stole the original scroll. He found his family home in poor condition, and realized that the treasure could be of use to the present generation even though he himself had no use for it. For a whole year he devoted himself to deciphering the scroll - calculating where the hidden treasure lay. Again he became madly engrossed in it. That is why he had not realized that in the past few days someone - Mrityunjaya - had been following him about.

"I have deciphered the final clue now and that is why I had screamed out "Got it" when you threw that stone at me", said Shankara. "If I want to, I can lead you to a treasure that even emperors do not possess. I can do it this instant."

Mrityunjaya grabbed hold of Shankara's feet. "Oh, do take me there!"

"The stone that you threw at me has killed - not me - but the last shreds of desire I still had left in me", said Shankara. "I have seen how desire can be a killer."

"You may be free from desire", pleaded Shankara." I am not. You cannot deprive me of the treasure!"

"Take your scroll back then. If you can hunt the treasure out, do take it." With this the mendicant placed the scroll near Mrityunjaya and his stick, and left.

"Oh, don't leave me here!" screamed Mrityunjaya. "Take pity on me. Show me where the treasure is."

There was no reply.

Leaning on the stick, Mrityunjaya tried to limp out. But the network of tunnels was too intricate. After a while, he collapsed wherever he was and fell asleep. When he awoke he felt so hungry that he ate some puffed rice that he had still left with him. He tried again to get out, but could not find the way. "O mendicant, where are you? "he screamed out.

The scream echoed along the underground tunnels and there floated back a reply: " I am close by. What do you want?"

"Kindly take me to the treasure", prayed Mrityunjaya.

There was no reply to that. Mrityunjaya cried again and again. But no one answered.

Again the fatigued fellow fell asleep and again he woke up in the dark." Are you there?" he screamed.

"I am here itself. Tell me what you want."

"Just take me out of this dark tunnel. I want nothing else."

" You don't want the treasure?"

"No, I don't", said Mrityunjaya.

There was the sound of flintstones being struck. Soon the mendicant became visible, holding a flare.

"Come, then, Mrityunjaya, let's get out of the tunnel", said the mendicant.

"Baba, is it all going to be a futile hunt? Even after all this, can't I get the treasure?"

Immediately the flare went out. "How cruel!" said Mrtiyunjaya and sat down again. There was no way he could measure the passage of time or find an end to the darkness stretching out in all directions. He felt like smashing up the darkness with all the force of body and mind that he had. He became desperate for light and air and the world outside.

"O cruel mendicant, I don't want the treasure. Rescue me."

"You don't want the treasure? Then take my hand. Come with me." No flare was lit, but Mrityunjaya could catch hold of the mendicant and limp forward with the help of the stick. For a long time they wound their way through dark passages and tunnels. Then there was the sound of a rusted iron door opening, and Mrityunjaya went ahead into some sort of a cell or room.

A little while later as the flare got lit, an amazing sight met his eyes. Across the wall there were thick sheets of shining gold – layers and layers of them!

Eyes glittering, Mritunjaya shouted out, "This gold is mine! I just cannot go leaving it behind."

"Alright then, don't", and the mendicant left him there with water, some puffed rice and a flare. He closed the iron door from outside.

Mrityunjaya felt the gold all around him, pulled some sheets out, put them in his lap, sounded them against one another, and then rubbed them all over his body.

Finally he laid the sheets of gold out on the floor like a mattress, and went to sleep on them. When he got up, he found gold shining down on him from all the sides. There was nothing else other than gold.

Mrityunjaya began to think. Perhaps it was morning outside; he remembered the morning smells and sounds. At home perhaps this moment the ducks were waddling down to the pond, and the maid washing the brass and copper utensils in its waters.

"Are you there, mendicant", Mrityunjaya hit the door from inside and called out.

The mendicant came in. "What do you want?" he asked. "I do want to go out. But can't I take just a couple of these sheets of gold?"

In answer, the mendicant just replenished his stock of

puffed rice and water, and went out. The door was locked once more.

Mrityunjaya took a thin sheet of gold and crumpled it into small pieces. He flung those pieces out like clods of earth. He bit into a few pieces of gold, making teeth marks. He stamped upon them again and again and tired himself out into sleep.

Waking up, again he saw the gold heaped all around him –. He again pounded on the door and shouted out, "Oh mendicant, I do not want the gold - I do not!"

But the door did not open. Mrityunjaya's voice got cracked with all the shouting. But the door remained closed.

Mrityunjaya picked up the pieces of gold and flung them upon the door. Nothing happened, Was the mendicant then gone? Was he never going to come back? Was he himself to remain confined in this golden prison forever and die by small degrees?

He felt terrified by the sight of so much gold around him. Cold and cruel, the gold had no throb of life in it. In the perpetual darkness of the underground, it was perpetually bright.

Was it evening now on earth? Mrityunjaya remembered the gold of sunset and of lamplight. Everyday scenes crowded into his brain – the grocery in Dharagol, his own home, the villagers going to the market, his pet dog curling up in the courtyard. If only he could go up and draw a breath of the fresh air!

Just then the door opened.

"What do you want, Mrityunjaya?" asked the mendicant. "I just want to get out of this maze of tunnels, this prison of gold. I want light, air and sky."

"There are stores of jewels here – worth much more than this store of gold. Won't you just take a look at them?"

"No", declared Mrityunjaya.

"Don't you want to just see them?"

"No, I don't even want to see them. I'd beg all my life rather than spend another moment here."

"Come then". The mendicant took him out of the room and led him to the mouth of the well with the chain. He handed him the scroll. "What do you want to do with this now?"

In answer Mrityunjaya tore it up and threw it into the well.

❐

17

Bequeathing the Property

Sampatti-Samarpan

"I am leaving!" A furious Vrindavan Kundu said to his father Yajnanath Kundu.

"Look at the fellow's ingratitude!" said the father. "Instead of repaying me for feeding and clothing him all this time, he is showing me his temper!"

Yajnanath Kundu could not have incurred much expense in feeding and clothing his son because he was a big miser. He hardly spent any money, even on essentials. The son had borne it quietly while he was unmarried. But after his marriage, he began to have ideas other than those of frugality that his father cherished. His wife fell ill and the physician recommended a very expensive medicine. Yajnanath called him inexperienced and made him leave. Vrindavan's wife died. Vrindavan blamed his father for her death. He felt that he would not have lost his wife if his father had paid for the medicine recommended.

"I am leaving!" he told his father after a fight.

His father instantly declared in public that he would never give Vrindavan a penny.

Father and son parted ways.

He did not miss his son much. In fact, he had always been a little scared that his son might poison him one day. With his daughter-in-law dying and his son leaving home, he felt relieved on this score. Also, there was a reduction in expenditure.

Only, he was hurt at losing his grandson, four-year-old Gokul. He cost very little to be fed and clothed and so his grandfather's affection for him was less encumbered. When Vrindavan had taken Gokul away with him, Yajnanath had felt genuine sorrow, but it had also struck him that he would now be relieved of the expenses of bringing Gokul up.

He missed his grandson a lot. No one now pestered him while he was doing his daily rituals, no one ran away with his pen and paper just when he was about to do his calculation of household expenses. The sight of Gokul's torn blanket and ink-marked mat tugged at his heart. Within two years that kid had torn his clothes to tatters. Yajnanath had scolded him severely then. Now those tatters brought tears to his eyes. Instead of using them to roll wicks for lamps and so save money, Yajnanath now locked them up in the safe. He resolved not to reproach Gokul even if he ruined his clothes again and again, provided he came back.

But Gokul never came back. Yajnanath seemed to grow old faster than before, when Gokul had been around. Every day when the village took its mid-day nap, he roamed restlessly around. The village lads teased him for his miserliness and called him names, so that he could hear.

One afternoon, while taking his usual walk in the shade of the mango grove, Yajnanath saw that a new boy – not of this village – had somehow assumed leadership of the village kids. He was teaching them new pranks and showing them new ways of mischief-making and they were accepting him as the head of their gang.

On other days, the kids ran away on seeing Yajnanath

approach. Today they came up to him and once close enough, shook a shawl almost upon his body. Out jumped a chameleon which quickly ran up his body before jumping off into the bushes. Yajnanath shivered and cowered back; the boys shouted in delight. Yajnanath walked on, but suddenly found the towel upon his shoulder vanish and adorn the head of the new boy.

For a long time Yajnanath had not tasted such unabashed intimacy with a kid.

He called the boy up. After a lot of invitations and assurances, the boy answered his questions.

"What is your name?"

"Nitai Pal."

"Where is your home?"

"Won't tell."

"What is your father's name?"

"Won't tell."

"Why?"

"Because I have run away from home."

"Why?"

"Because my father wants to send me to school".

The father is certainly a fool to be sending such a son to school, thought Yajnanath. He offered the boy his own home to stay in. The boy took up the offer without a trace of hesitation. In fact, as days went by, he stayed on as though it was his own. In matters of food and clothing he expressed his preferences with such flourish that Yajnanath had to admit defeat and fulfill all his demands. He called Yajnanath `Dada', that is, Grand-pa. Neighbours grew envious of the boy's luck in finding such a patron because Yajnanath was reputed to be very rich. They felt that Yajnanath's end was near and before dying, he would bequeath all his wealth upon Nitai.

There were times when Nitai threatened to go away. Yajnanath would then tell him, "Child, when I pass away, I shall leave all my property to you."

Young as he was, Nitai appreciated the worth of this assurance. The villagers, jealous of Nita's prospects, began to inquire after his father. "How worried his parents must be!" they said. "The kid too is a rogue."

One day Yajnanath came to hear from a passer by that someone named Damodar Pal was coming this way, looking for his son. Nitai got most upset at hearing this. He got ready to run off, leaving all the property he had been promised.

Yajnanath assured him: "I'll hide you in such a place that nobody will be able to find you out. Not even the villagers."

Curious, Nitai asked to be shown the place. Yajnanath answered that if he took him there now, others would get to know about it. He would take Nitai there at night. Nitai cheered up at the thought of this new mystery. What fun, he thought that his father would come to this very village but be unable to find him! Also, what a good hiding place he would have for his games of hide-and-seek with the village kids!

At mid-day, Yajnanath locked Nitai up in the house and went away somewhere. As soon as he came back, Nitai began to pester him with his questions. Evening fell; Nitai grew was impatient to be taken to his hiding-place.

"It is not yet dark", Yajnanath stalled.

"It is dark, Dada", persisted Nitai. "Let's go."

"The neighbours are not yet asleep", Yajnanath stalled again.

Nitai grew tired and sleepy as the night grew deeper and darker. Finally, at midnight, Yajnanath took him by the hand and led him out through the sleeping village, with the stray dogs barking after them. Crossing over many fields, they arrived at a jungle with a ruined temple in its midst.

"Here?" said Nitai, a little disappointed. He had come across several such ruins in the course of his wanderings. It was a good place for playing hide-and-seek, but nothing great.

Then Yajnanath lifted up a block of stone from the floor of the ruined temple. Nitai caught sight of a small room below, lit by a lamp. He was most surprised and also a little scared. Using a ladder, Yajnanath climbed down and Nitai fearfully followed him.

Once below, he saw that all around the small room there were metal pots. In the middle of the room there was a mat, and before it were materials for the worship of a deity, such as sandalwood paste, vermilion, and flower garlands. To satisfy his curiosity, Nitai looked into a pot. It was full of coins of gold and silver.

"Nitai, I had told you that I would leave all my property to you. This is all that I have and I am going to bequeath it upon you."

Nitai jumped up and asked, "All of it? You don't want a single coin for yourself?"

"No", said Yajnanath. "But there is something I have to say. If my lost grandson Gokul ever comes back, or his son, or his grandson or any descendant, you have to make all this over to him, every single coin of it."

The boy thought that Yajnanath had gone mad. He easily answered, "Alright".

"Then come and sit on the mat", said Yajnanath. "You have to be worshipped".

"Why?"

"That is the procedure".

The boy took his seat upon the mat. Yajnanath anointed his forehead with sandalwood paste and put a dot of vermilion on it. He hung a garland round his neck, sat down in front of him and began to mutter some mantra in a low voice.

Getting worshipped like a deity and listening to that incantation, Nitai grew scared. "Dada," he called.

Yajnanath did not reply but went on with his incantation.

At last, with difficulty and one by one, he began to draw the heavy metal pots close and place them before Nitai. He dedicated each of them to Nitai, but every time he made him say:

"I will hand over in exact number all these coins to the son, grandson or any further descendant of Gokul Chandra Kundu, son of Vrindavan Kundu, son of Yajnanath Kundu, son of Paramanand Kundu, son of Prankrishna Kundu, son of Gadadhar Kundu, son of Yudhisthira Kundu ...."

Reciting this list again and again, Nitai grew baffled and confused. His tongue gradually grew stiff, his voice indistinct. By the time the ceremony was over, the small room was full of vapour from the lamp and the breath of both of them. The boy's mouth grew dry, his hands and feet began to tingle and he felt choked.

The lamp grew dim and went out. In the dark, the boy could feel Yajnanath going up the ladder.

"Where are you going, Dada?" he cried out in anguish.

"I am going", Yajnanath called down. "You stay here – nobody will be able to find you But remember, Gokul Chandra Kundu, son of Vrindavan Kundu, son of Yajnanath Kundu."

With this, he reached the top and immediately pulled the ladder up. His breath coming to a halt, the boy uttered with great difficulty: "Dada, I want to go to Baba."

Yajnanath placed the block of stone on the hole and strained his ears to hear Nitai call out once more in a choking voice: " Bab—".There was the sound of a fall and no other sound after that. (Thus Yajnanath bequeathed his property to a *yaksha.* In Indian mythology, the *yaksha*s are guards of Kubera, the treasurer of the gods).Yajnanath began to cover up the block of stone with earth, and cover it up further with bricks and sand from the crumbling temple. He then planted creepers on it and even though the night was almost over, did not seem to be able to move from the spot. Every now and then he put his ear to the ground. He seemed to hear a cry rising from the depth of the earth. As if to choke off that cry, he restlessly piled more and more earth upon the temple floor. But wasn't there someone still crying out `Baba'?"

Stamping on the ground Yajnanath said, "Stop it! Everyone will hear you."

But still there was a cry of 'Baba'.

Yajnanath looked around and found it was broad daylight. Scared, he came away from that jungle into the open fields.

There too he could hear someone crying`Baba'. Startled, Yajnanath turned round to find his own son Vrindavan there. "Baba", he said, "I got the information that my son is hiding in your house. Hand him over."

"Your son?" Puckering up his face and eyes, Yajnanath bent over upon Vrindavan.

"Yes, Gokul", replied Vrindavan. "Now he is called Nitai Pal. Everywhere around this place, people know of you as a miser and avoid pronouncing your name. So out of shame we had changed our names."

With his ten fingers Yajnanath clutched at the air and fell down. When he regained his consciousness, he dragged Vrindavan to the temple. "Can you hear anyone crying?' he asked.

"No", said Vrindavan. The old man seemed to be very relieved.

Since then, he went round asking everybody if they could hear anybody crying. People considered him mad and laughed at him. Within four years, he approached his end. It grew dark around him and he found it difficult to breathe. At the last moment, he suddenly sat up, groped in the air, and cried out: "Nitai, who took away my ladder?"

Then, with a thud, he fell down dead on the bed, going to the hiding place from which no one ever could be found out.

❑❑❑

Glossary

Anchal—one end of the sari, covering the breast and the head

Baba—father

Babu—honorific for a superior or more powerful person used in Bengal

Bhanshee—bamboo flute

Bata—Banyan tree

Dada—respectful term for an elder brother or grandfather

Dada-babu—an elder especially to be respected, usually an young employer

Dhoti—stretch of cloth wrapped around lower part of body, main dress of Bengali men

Guru-deva—preceptor seen as a deity

Jatra—moving play performance

Jorasanko—Tagore's ancestral place in Kolkata (Calcutta)

Kaka—uncle, father's brother

Khoka-babu—young master, term of respect(babu) applied to a male child(khoka)

Khonkhi—khuku(girl) pronounced by Kabuliwala

Kavi-guru—preceptor of poets

Nayeb—adminsitrative officer serving the local landlord

Padma—important river, now in Bangladesh

Paglee—feminine form of pagal or mad, often affectionately used

Pagol(Pagal)—mad

Pan—vow, promise to be kept

Panchan—bitter herbal drink

Paan—Betel leaf folded over betel-nut and a few other ingredients

Rabindra—Bharati-university built on Tagore's ancestral place in Kolkata

Santiniketan—a place on Bengal-Bihar border where Tagore experimented with education

Sari—a long stretch of beautiful cloth that Bengali women drape around themselves as their main dress

Sasur-bari—residence of in-laws , the ***bari*** or home of every woman after her marriage

Shimul—silk-cotton tree

Suttee/Sati—daha-pratha- system of immolating widows

Tantrik—ascetic practicing Tantra rituals

Tentul—Tamarind tree

Visva Bharati—university developed from Tagore's experimental school at Santiniketan

Zamindar(Jomidar)—landlord collecting tax from Bengal villagers and submitting it to British officers under the Permanent Settlement Act 1793, abolished after Independence